Healthy Eating for Babies & Toddlers

Healthy Eating
for Babies
& Toddlers

Anne Sheasby and Jill Scott
with Kathleen M. Zelman

CLB

4959
This edition published in 1998 by CLB
Copyright © 1998 Quadrillion Publishing Ltd.
Woolsack Way, Godalming, Surrey, GU7 1XW
Distributed in the USA by Quadrillion Publishing Inc.,
230 Fifth Avenue, New York, NY 10001

ISBN 1-85833-399-7

Printed and bound in Singapore

Nutrition Consultant: Kathleen M. Zelman
Design Management: Justina Leitão
Additional Design: Peter Laws
Editorial: Beverly LeBlanc
Photography: Sheila Terry
Additional Photography: Jeremy Thomas
Illustration: Mark Buckingham
Home Economy: Anne Sheasby
Production: Neil Randles and Ruth Arthur

AUTHORS' ACKNOWLEDGMENTS

The authors would like to thank Robert, Ian, and Emily for their on-going support and encouragement with this book and for their tireless tasting of all the recipes; to John and Sheila Terry for their hard work and patience on the food photography; and to Peter B. Ledbury Ltd, Wantage, England, for the loan of kitchen equipment for photography.

contents

introduction *10*

C H A P T E R 1
4 –6 Months
Getting Started *16*

C H A P T E R 2
6 –9 Months
the Second Stage *38*

C H A P T E R 3
9 –12 Months
Moving on to Family Foods *58*

C H A P T E R 4
1–5 Years
Healthy eating For toddlers *78*

C H A P T E R 5
1–5 Years
Parties and Picnics *102*

Nutritional information *122*
index *125*

INTRODUCTION

If you enjoy your food, and would like your children to develop a taste for healthy, delicious food, this book is for you. If you would like practical tips and helpful advice about feeding babies and toddlers, read on. And, if you are looking for easy-to-prepare, tasty, and nutritious recipes for your baby from 4 months to 5 years of age, you'll find more than 100 of them in the following pages.

What's special about babies and toddlers?

Infants and young children are unique in lots of ways, not least because of their high nutritional needs. They go through periods of rapid growth and development. For example, your baby will probably increase in length by 10 inches (25 cm) in her first year, and will probably have doubled her birth weight by the time she is 6 months old. Thereafter, she will continue to grow and develop, providing she gets all the energy (calories) and essential nutrients she needs.

There's also some scientific evidence to suggest that a healthy diet at this early age can help to protect your child from many of today's "adult" diseases, such as heart disease. Therefore, it's important to establish good eating habits right from the start.

Before reading the following chapters, have a look at the information on the next few pages, to help you understand more about what we mean by "healthy eating" for babies and toddlers, and to find out how to make the most of this book.

"Healthy eating" for babies and toddlers

Most of us have some idea about the main food and health messages for adults. We

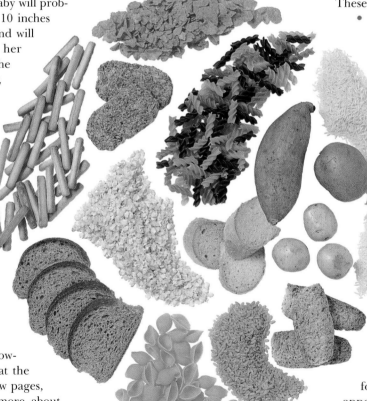

know that eating too much fat is linked to heart disease, for example, and that fresh fruit and vegetables can help protect us against diseases, such as heart disease, and some cancers. But what about young children? Should we be restricting fat intake at an early age? What does

"healthy eating" mean for babies and toddlers? It means offering your child a healthy balance of foods which contain the essential nutrients she needs.

These include:
- starchy carbohydrate foods, such as bread, pasta, rice, cereals, and potatoes, for energy (calories) and other nutrients
- fruit and vegetables for vitamins and minerals
- foods containing protein, such as meat, fish, eggs, beans, and legumes, for growth and development
- milk and dairy foods for healthy bones and teeth

In addition to the foods above, there are other nutrients to mention, so let's take a closer look at some of these.

Fats

Fat is an excellent source of energy (calories), particularly for babies and toddlers, whose appetites can be small but energy requirements high. Low-fat diets are not appropriate for very young children because they may not get all the calories they need to grow, especially children under the age of 2 years. During this age period, choose full-fat varieties of dairy products.

Between the ages of 2 and 5, as your child gradually moves toward an adult diet, you can start to introduce some lower-fat varieties of foods, such as low-fat milk, low-fat yogurts, and so on, providing she is gaining weight well and eating a variety of foods every day. At this stage, starchy foods (bread, pasta, rice, and potatoes) should become a more important source of calories than fat.

Types of fat

Choose a pure vegetable oil, such as sunflower, olive, or corn oil, for use in cooking, since these oils are a good source of essential fats. For spreading or baking, there is a wide choice available. In the recipes, we suggest either butter or margarine, or use whatever the usual family spread is, provided it is suitable for cooking or baking with.

It's worth remembering, however, that for long-term health, it's a good idea to cut down on saturated fat, because it is the type of fat that has been linked with heart disease. Buy spreads which are lower in saturated fat and high in either monounsaturates or polyunsaturates. These are the healthier types of fat.

Sugars

There are lots of different types of sugars, which provide energy but do not contain any other nutrients. Some sugars naturally occur in foods, such as lactose in milk, and fruit sugar (fructose) in whole fruits and vegetables. These foods (milk, fruits, and vegetables) do provide valuable nutrients, and should be an important part of your child's daily diet (see specific chapters for quantities of these foods to offer at different ages).

All sugars can potentially cause tooth decay, and because young children are at risk, it's a good idea to pay attention to your child's dental health from the start. We discuss this further in Chapter 4, but one of the key messages for tooth decay prevention is to limit high-sugar foods and drinks, especially between meals. It is advisable not to let your baby go to bed with a bottle containing anything other than water. Nutrient-laden liquid pools in a baby's mouth can cause tooth decay and are a breeding ground for bacteria.

In some of the recipes, we've used small amounts of sugar, where necessary, to make foods more acceptable, such as stewed plums, or where the recipe dictates, such as for cake baking. In many recipes, we suggest using ripe fruit in season, which is naturally sweet, and recommend canned fruit in natural juice, which tastes less sweet than fruit in syrup.

Honey

Honey is often suggested as a "healthier" alternative to sugar, perhaps because it tastes sweeter than sugar and therefore less can be used in cooking. Honey, however, is just as harmful to teeth as other sugars, but there is another nutritional concern about giving honey to babies under the age of 12 months.

Experts recommend that honey should not be given to babies under 12 months of age, because of the small risk of bacterial infection. Occasionally, honey may contain naturally occurring bacterial spores which are not removed during processing. These are harmless to older children and adults, but young children are more at risk of illness because their intestines are not developed enough to cope with the bacteria. Commercially manufactured weaning foods containing honey are not affected in the same way because of the processing they undergo.

Salt

A small amount of sodium (salt) is essential to good health for babies as well as adults. Babies, however, are not able to deal with an excess of sodium, since their kidneys are not fully developed, so their salt intake should be limited. Don't add salt to your baby's food, especially in the first year, and watch out for highly salted foods, such as bacon and other cured meats; potato chips and savory snacks; some canned foods. Because of the highly sensitive nature of babies' taste buds, they don't need it anyway.

Some foods are naturally high in salt, such as cheese, so if you are serving cheese at a meal, try to avoid offering another high-salt food at the same time. Choose fresh vegetables and potatoes with the cheese, followed by stewed or fresh fruit. It's really a question of balance at mealtimes.

Too much dietary salt is linked to high blood pressure in adults, so why not review your intake of salt and try to cut down the amount used in cooking and at the table for the whole family?

We've not added salt to any of the recipes and have included our own recipes for homemade stocks (see pages 14–15) to use in place of bouillon cubes or granules, which are too salty for babies and young children. In a few recipes, we've included small amounts of tomato ketchup, tomato paste, or Worcestershire sauce, for flavor. These ingredients are high in salt, so use sparingly in dishes for young children.

Fiber

Grains, such as brown rice, whole-wheat pasta, and whole-wheat bread, along with fruits and vegetables, are good sources of fiber, as well as vitamins and minerals. Dietary fiber is important in the diet for healthy digestive systems, so include some of these foods in your child's meals. But don't go for overload—cereal foods can be very bulky. If she fills up on bulky foods, your child may not be able to eat enough foods to provide all the calories she needs. Some high-fiber foods also contain substances which can prevent or slow down the absorption of essential minerals, such as iron and zinc. When adding fiber to a young person's diet, it is important to understand not only will it fill up the child, but it will cause gas and bloating, which are uncomfortable. Introduce whole grains slowly and gradually along with plenty of fluids.

To sum up, the key message about fiber is: offer a mixture of cereal foods, some whole-grain varieties, some white, and don't include too much fiber when your child is under 2 years old. Include plenty of fresh fruit and vegetables, alongside other foods

To increase the fiber content of this dish (Pasta Twists with Zucchini, page 69), use all whole-wheat pasta or a mixture of white and whole-wheat pasta.

essential for growth and development (see specific chapters for recommended amounts at different ages). In the recipes, we use a mixture of whole-wheat and processed varieties of pasta and rice.

Vitamins and minerals
Vitamins and minerals are needed in small amounts, and should be provided in the diet on a daily basis. This is particularly important for young children and babies to meet growing demands. Between 6–12 months and 1–3 years are the times when nutritional needs for certain minerals, especially iron, are high, so including foods which are good sources of iron is important. We discuss this in more detail in chapters 2 and 4.

Vitamin C helps the absorption of iron from cereal and vegetable sources, so a regular intake of this vitamin at mealtimes is particularly beneficial (see the guide to recipe symbols on page 13).

Vitamin supplements
Your physician may recommend vitamin supplements. Additionally, often breast-fed babies require vitamin D oral floride.

Food allergies
If we were writing this book a few years ago, there probably wouldn't be the need for a paragraph on food allergies. Nowadays, however, it seems that more babies and young children are showing some adverse reaction to certain foods. Children under 3 years have the highest number of allergies and often outgrow them with time. The most commonly

occurring allergies in infants, in descending order, are: cows' milk, eggs, peanuts, tree nuts, soybeans, and wheat.

Food allergy can cause or contribute to the development of eczema, asthma, hay fever, skin rashes, or digestive disorders (especially diarrhea).

It is recommended you introduce new foods every other day to infants, regardless of family history of allergies. If you are concerned about food allergy, speak to your pediatrician or a dietitian before excluding foods from your baby's diet.

Reducing the risk of food allergies
• If you are breast-feeding, try to continue until your baby is at least 4–6 months old, and preferably longer.
• Wait until your baby is at least 4 months old before introducing any solids into her diet, and avoid including potentially allergic foods until she is at least 6 months old. These foods include: whole cows' milk, eggs, wheat, nuts, citrus fruits, soybeans, and fresh tomatoes.

Other nonfood allergens should also be avoided, such as cigarette and cigar smoke, excessive house dust, and close contact with pets.

Choking dangers
All round foods, such as hot dogs, carrots, hard candies, peanuts, and other types of nut should not be fed to infants or young children because of the risk of causing them to choke.

Peanuts
Peanuts need a special mention because peanuts and peanut products can cause a rare but severe reaction in sensitive children and adults. Symptoms can appear in minutes, and immediate hospital treatment is required. Seek advice from your pediatrician or a dietitian.

HOW TO USE THIS BOOK

We have divided the book into five chapters, covering the different stages of weaning, healthy eating for toddlers, and parties and picnics. Simply turn to the required chapter, read a little more about your child's nutritional needs, and try out the delicious recipes, all of which have been tried and tested and many of which have been enjoyed by Emily, Jill's baby daughter.

GUIDE TO THE RECIPES

• Both standard American cups and metric measurements are given in each recipe in the book. Use one set of measurements only, either cups or metric, because they are not interchangeable.

    1 tablespoon = one 15 ml spoon
    1 teaspoon = one 5 ml spoon

• Ovens and broilers should be preheated to the temperature specified in the recipe. The cooking times for all the recipes are based on the oven or broiler being preheated. If using a fan oven, follow the manufacturer's instructions for adjusting the time and temperature.

• In the recipes, we've used the conventional cooking methods. Steaming rather than boiling vegetables is a good alternative, and if you have a microwave oven, you can use it for cooking and reheating foods to save time. Always follow the manufacturer's directions when using microwave ovens.

• All eggs used in the recipes are large. It is recommended that eggs are cooked until solid (both egg yolk and white) before serving to young children, especially under 12 months.

• All the recipes included in this book are suitable for freezing, unless otherwise stated. Food deep frozen at -64°F/ -18°C may be kept for up to 3 months.

• Finely chopped fresh herbs are used in many of the recipes in the book. Dried herbs can be used instead, but fresh herbs give a better flavor. Approximately 1 tbsp. (15 ml) of chopped fresh herbs is the equivalent of 1 teaspoon of dried herbs.

• The number of portions suggested in the recipes throughout the book are for babies and young children. These are approximate, and should only be used as a guide, because serving sizes will vary from baby to baby.

• The quantities of ingredients in all the recipes can easily be increased to make a meal for all the family to enjoy.

• All vegetables and fruit used in the recipes should be thoroughly washed under cold running water before using. We suggest peeling all vegetables and fruit for babies in their first year.

GUIDE TO THE RECIPE SYMBOLS

Throughout the book, you will notice a number of symbols and notes underneath each of the recipes. These are explained in the table to the right.

🏵: Yes
This recipe is suitable for vegetarians.

🏵: No
This recipe is not suitable for vegetarians.

❄: Yes
This recipe is suitable for freezing.

❄: No
This recipe is not suitable for freezing.

To make sure you are including sufficient iron-containing foods in your child's diet, look for these symbols:

Iron: ▲
This recipe is a useful source of iron.

Iron: ▲▲
This recipe is a rich source of iron.

Vitamin C aids the absorption of iron from nonmeat sources.

Vitamin C: ▲
This recipe is a useful source of vitamin C.

Vitamin C: ▲▲
This recipe is a rich source of vitamin C.

Calcium is an essential mineral for the growth and development of healthy bones and teeth. Look for these symbols as a guide to calcium content:

Calcium: ▲
This recipe is a useful source of calcium.

Calcium: ▲▲
This recipe is a rich source of calcium.

▲
An average serving size will provide more than one sixth of the Recommended Dietary Allowance of this mineral or vitamin for babies and young children.

▲▲
An average serving size will provide over 50% of the Recommended Dietary Allowance of this vitamin or mineral for babies and young children.

HOMEMADE STOCKS

You really can't beat the flavor of homemade stocks, and they are simple to make. They are particularly good for using in food prepared for babies and young children, because you can control the amount of seasoning you add to the soup, avoiding the risk of giving excess salt to your child.

A wide range of stock and bouillon products are available, including bouillon cubes, bouillon granules, and fresh, chilled stock, but many of them are strong in flavor and excessively salty. Therefore, you should avoid feeding them to babies and toddlers.

These homemade stocks are also delicious used for creating recipes for adults. And, once you have started to make your own stocks, there will be no looking back! We suggest making one or two batches of stock and freezing them in useful quantities for future use. Freeze homemade stocks for up to 3 months.

CHICKEN STOCK
Makes about 2³/₄ cups (700 ml)

1 meaty chicken carcass

6 shallots or 1 onion

1 carrot

2 celery stalks

1 bay leaf

1 Break or chop the chicken carcass into pieces and place in a large saucepan with 7 cups (1.7 liters) cold water.

2 Peel and slice the shallots or onion and carrot, and chop the celery. Add to the saucepan with the bay leaf. Stir to mix.

3 Bring to a boil, then partially cover and simmer for about 2 hours, skimming off any scum and fat which rises to the surface during cooking.

4 Strain the stock through a strainer, then set the liquid aside to cool.

5 When cold, remove and discard all the fat and use or freeze as required.

BEEF STOCK
Makes about 2³/₄ cups (700 ml)

1 lb. (450 g) shin of beef on the bone

1 lb. (450 g) beef or veal bones

1 onion

1 carrot

1 turnip

2 celery stalks

1 leek, cleaned

1 bouquet garni

1 Place the meat and bones in a roasting pan and brown in a preheated oven at 425°F (220°C) for about 30 minutes. Transfer to a large saucepan with 2 quarts (1.7 liters) cold water.

2 Peel and slice the onion and carrot; peel and dice the turnip; chop the celery and leek. Add to the saucepan with the bouquet garni. Stir to mix.

3 Bring to a boil, then partially cover and simmer for about 2 hours, skimming off any scum and fat which rises to the surface during cooking.

4 Strain the stock through a strainer, then set the strained liquid aside. Allow to cool thoroughly.

5 When cold, remove and discard all the fat and use or freeze as required.

VEGETABLE STOCK
Makes about 5¹/₄ cups (1.3 liters)

1 large onion, sliced

2 carrots, sliced

1 leek, sliced

3 celery stalks, chopped

1 small turnip, diced

1 small parsnip, sliced

1 bouquet garni

1 Place all the prepared vegetables in a large saucepan with the bouquet garni. Add 2 quarts (1.7 liters) cold water and stir to mix thoroughly.

2 Bring to the boil, then partially cover and simmer for 1–1¹/₂ hours, skimming off any scum which rises to the surface during the cooking time.

3 Strain the stock through a strainer, then set the liquid aside to cool thoroughly. Use or freeze as required.

Vegetable stock can be made using many mixtures of vegetables. If you have any vegetable trimmings—such as tomato skins, celery tops, or cabbage leaves—add those to the vegetables and water. Or use more unusual vegetable mixtures such as sweet potatoes, shallots, rutabaga, Jerusalem artichokes, and a bunch of fresh herbs.

CHAPTER 1

4–6 MONTHS

Getting Started

As a parent, starting the weaning process with your first baby is a whole new experience. In fact, it is a time of learning and exploration for both you and your baby. It can be fun and often rewarding trying out new tastes and textures, but it can also be a time of uncertainty if you are preparing your own baby food for the first time.

Your main concerns will probably be centered around how confident you feel about following the right guidelines and doing what is best for your baby. In the following introduction to this chapter, we present those guidelines clearly and concisely so that you can begin weaning with a truly positive frame of mind.

WEANING WITHOUT WORRY

The most common worries parents usually have about weaning are: Is my baby eating enough? How much milk should I offer at first? (This is particularly difficult if you are breast-feeding.) When should I start? What foods should I offer? Do all the feeding utensils need to be sterilized? We set out to provide the answers to these key questions, to make the whole experience of weaning more enjoyable and less stressful.

When to wean?

For the first few months, breast milk or infant formula provides all the nourishment your baby needs. From about the age of 4 to 6 months, however, solids should be introduced to babies. By this age, the digestive system is mature enough to cope with the weaning diet, babies are ready developmentally, and they begin to need the extra energy and nutrients to meet growing demands.

Every baby is different, and there is no need to rush into giving her solids. At this stage, you are just introducing different tastes and textures in small amounts. Milk will still provide most of the nutrients your baby needs.

Home-prepared meals or commercial baby foods, or both?

Most people provide their baby with a mixture of home-prepared foods and commercial baby foods. When you make your own dishes, you know exactly what's in them, you can vary the textures more easily, and feel satisfied if your baby enjoys it. Commercial baby foods are useful when you are out and about or need to provide an instant meal for your hungry baby. Most of them are fortified with vitamins and minerals to replace those lost in processing, so they do provide a balanced meal.

You can also combine home-made foods with commercial baby foods in the same meal, for example adding mashed potato to a jar or can of a savory food, or preparing a custard sauce to add to a jar of puréed fruit.

In this first chapter, we show how you can prepare almost any combination of fruits and vegetables quickly and easily, to offer a wide variety of different tastes to your baby at this early stage.

What you need to get started

You don't need any special equipment, just a few basic items, as follows:
- a plastic weaning bowl or bowls, and a weaning spoon or spoons
- a plastic strainer or baby food mill
- an electric blender or food processor —the quick and easy way to purée fruits and vegetables
- ice-cube trays, freezer bags, and labels, for storing food if you have a freezer

Good hygiene is an important consideration before you start weaning, because young babies can easily pick

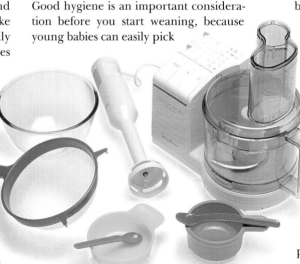

up infections. Follow the guidelines below to help protect your baby:
- Always wash your hands thoroughly before you begin handling any food and feeding equipment.
- Sterilize as much of your baby's feeding equipment as possible, including weaning bowls and spoons, bottles, and so on, until your baby is at least 6 months old.
- Keep all other feeding and cooking utensils scrupulously clean.
- Remember to use separate chopping boards for meat and poultry and fruit and vegetables.

It's a good idea to buy some baby rice, because this is useful for adding calories to puréed fruits and vegetables; a variety of fresh and frozen fruit and vegetables; canned fruits packed in natural juice, and then you're ready to begin! Look at the recipes we've suggested in this chapter before going shopping so that you can stock up on the fruits and vegetables we've used. Try experimenting with your own combinations of fruit and vegetables.

It's worth spending an hour or so in the kitchen (baby permitting!) preparing a batch of different recipes and freezing them so that you have a selection of foods to choose from at mealtimes. It really does help to be organized and prepared in advance, particularly in the first few weeks of weaning your baby.

TIPS ON PREPARING YOUR BABY'S FOOD

- Peel and pit or seed all fruit and vegetables at this stage.
- Cook vegetables in just enough boiling water to cover them. Remember to cook vegetables until soft, so they are easy to purée. Alternatively, vegetables can be steamed or cooked in a microwave oven until very tender.
- Use fresh fruits and vegetables in season. Alternatively, use canned fruit in natural juice or frozen fruits and vegetables out of season.
- Raw fruit, such as bananas, should be fully ripe before using in a recipe. Some fruit may need to be lightly cooked before being puréed.
- Frozen fruit and vegetables are just as nutritious as fresh varieties, and are useful at this stage because you are able to use such small amounts. A tablespoon of peas will be more than enough for a tasty meal, combined with mashed potato or sweet potato.
- When puréeing or straining cooked fruits or vegetables, add either a little of the cooking water, boiled water, home-made stock, or, for a creamier, more nutritious option, add enough of your baby's usual milk. This will help turn the mixture into a smooth paste.

TIPS ON SERVING YOUR BABY'S FOOD

- Babies are used to warm breast milk or infant formula, so it's a good idea to warm the food before serving at this stage. Do this either by standing the bowl in hot water, or heating it in a microwave oven. If you choose to use a microwave, always follow the manufacturers' directions. Make sure microwaved food is heated through by leaving it to stand for a few moments and stirring well before serving.
- Always test the temperature of the food on the back of your hand before serving any warm food to your baby.
- Only serve small amounts to start with; you can always increase the quantity of food you give to your baby if she still seems to be hungry.
- Any uneaten prepared food should always be discarded.
- Don't force-feed your baby—if she rejects the food, you might try one other flavor. Otherwise assume she isn't hungry, or simply does not want any food at that time.
- Offer just 1–2 teaspoons to your baby to start with, using a plastic baby spoon.

TIPS ON STORING YOUR BABY'S FOOD

- Preparing food in advance and storing it in the freezer saves time at mealtimes. If you have a variety of dishes or single portions of fruits and vegetables in the freezer, you know there is always a choice of foods to offer.
- Follow the recipe, blending the dish to the right consistency, then cool quickly, cover, and place in the refrigerator until cold. Transfer the food to sterilized ice-cube trays, cover with plastic wrap, or place in a sealed freezer bag, and freeze. A 1-tablespoon serving of homemade baby food will fill about 1 section of an ice-cube tray.
- Once frozen, the baby food can be removed from the ice-cube tray and stored in clearly labeled, clean freezer bags for up to 3 months.
- To defrost the frozen baby food, leave it covered in the refrigerator overnight. Alternatively, defrost thoroughly in a microwave oven. Foods such as cooked meat should be defrosted in the refrigerator, and not left to defrost at room temperature.
- When reheating, the food must be heated thoroughly until piping hot throughout, then leave to cool to the correct temperature.
- Defrosted food should be eaten on the same day and any leftovers thrown away. Never refreeze defrosted frozen food.
- Cooked food which is to be given to your baby later can be stored in the refrigerator for up to 24 hours.

INTRODUCING SOLIDS—WHEN AND WHAT TO TRY FIRST

In addition to the recipes suggested, it is useful to freeze single portions of cooked and puréed fruits and vegetables, such as carrots, pears, apples, and sweet potatoes, so that you always know you have something in the freezer for supper.

It's also a good idea to choose a time in the day when you and your baby are relaxed. Lunchtime is often a favorite

EARLY MORNING:
Breast milk or infant formula

MIDMORNING:
Breast milk or infant formula

LUNCH:
Breast milk or infant formula, plus 1 to 2 teaspoons baby rice mixed with breast milk or infant formula, or puréed fruits or vegetables

MIDAFTERNOON:
Breast milk or infant formula

BEDTIME:
Breast milk or infant formula

time to begin introducing solids (see the feeding guide above). To start with, just offer 1 to 2 teaspoons after a milk feed at one meal a day. As a guide, your feeding plan might be something like this: initially, offer single fruits and vegetables, on their own or mixed with a little baby rice or potato for extra energy (calories). Good first foods include any of the following fruits and vegetables: stewed apple; poached pear; mashed banana; puréed carrots, mashed potato, parsnips, cauliflower, and sweet potato.

Once your baby has become accustomed to the spoon, is familiar with a few foods, and does not have any adverse

reaction to any of them, try combining different tastes and textures. The food can start to be a little thicker from now on and slightly lumpier in texture, but still puréed. The recipes on the following pages will give you some ideas for appetizing combinations, and you can add some ideas of your own. For example, try carrot and apple, pear and carrot, and so on. Don't be surprised if your baby shows taste preferences even at this early age—they seem to know instinctively what they like! If she rejects a food, try serving it again in a week or two—she may have changed her mind.

Gradually introduce solids at more than one meal occasion, so that by 6 months, most babies will be eating some food at three mealtimes. Remember that every baby is different: some take to solids really quickly, others more slowly. So, enjoy your baby's individuality and don't rush her. As long as she is drinking plenty of milk, she will be getting all the nutrients she needs.

A typical daily feeding guide when your baby is around 5–6 months might be something like the guide on the right:

This is only a rough guide—all babies are different. Some will be eating a lot more than others at this stage, so let your baby be your guide.

The message for this chapter is: keep it simple! We've mentioned a number of suitable first foods, and developed some delicious recipes for them. When your baby has become accustomed to the first few foods, you can start introducing some foods with a little more protein and other nutrients in them, such as well-cooked meats and legumes. For example, we've used lentils in one dish. However, there are a number of foods which experts recommend should be

EARLY MORNING:
Breast milk or infant formula

BREAKFAST:
Breast milk or infant milk, plus baby rice with mashed fruit, such as banana, pear, or apricots

MIDMORNING:
Breast milk or infant formula

LUNCH:
Breast milk or infant formula, plus Green Bean, Zucchini, and Cheese Purée (page 29), followed by Fruit Cocktail Purée (page 34), if desired

MIDAFTERNOON:
Breast milk or infant formula

DINNER:
Baby Rice and Nectarine Purée (page 34)

BEDTIME:
Breast milk or infant formula

avoided at this stage because some babies might be prone to allergies. These are listed below.

FOODS TO AVOID AT THIS STAGE
- foods containing gluten, found in wheat, oats, barley, and rye, including bread, cereals, flour, pasta, and porridge
- eggs
- nuts
- fish

Many parents also choose to avoid feeding their babies citrus fruits and tomatoes in the first stage, because these foods can be allergenic in the case of certain individuals. Salt, sugar, and spices should not be added to foods at this stage.

In this chapter, we've chosen fresh vegetables for the recipes. Frozen vegetables are a good, tasty, and nutritious alternative to fresh ones, and are ideal to use when vegetables such as peas or spinach are out of season. Remember, if using frozen vegetables, once they are thawed and cooked, do not refreeze them.

MASHED POTATO WITH CARROTS

Makes about 18 tablespoons

Carrots are a wonderful first weaning food—they are sweet, brightly colored, and have a pleasant texture. Here we've combined carrots with potato, but they are also suitable on their own. Organic carrots have the best flavor.

Peel and dice 1 medium potato and 1 medium carrot. Place in a saucepan and cover with boiling water. Cover and simmer for 10–15 minutes, or until cooked and tender. Drain well, reserving some of the cooking liquid. Purée the vegetables in a blender with a little cooking liquid until smooth, or purée in a baby food mill, adding enough cooking liquid, boiled water, or baby milk (expressed breast milk or infant formula) to make the desired consistency. Alternatively, add a small amount of fresh cows' milk.

Useful Notes

❀: Yes   ❀: Yes

ROOT VEGETABLE PURÉE

Makes about 19 tablespoons

We have used a flavorful combination of sweet potato, turnip, and carrot for this purée, but try your own combination to vary the flavors. Other suitable root vegetables include rutabaga, parsnip, and celery root. Sweet potato is also delicious on its own, and babies often like the texture and taste of sweet potato better than an ordinary potato.

Peel and dice 1 medium sweet potato and 1 small turnip. Peel and thinly slice 1 small carrot. Place in a saucepan and cover with boiling water. Cover and simmer for 10–15 minutes, or until cooked and tender. Drain well, reserving some of the cooking liquid. Place the cooked vegetables in a blender and blend with a little cooking liquid until smooth, or purée in a baby food mill. Spoon the required amount into a bowl and add enough of the reserved cooking liquid or baby milk to make the desired consistency.

Useful Notes

❀: Yes   ❀: Yes

BABY RICE AND ZUCCHINI

Makes about 13 tablespoons

Baby rice is a useful thickener when using "watery" vegetables, such as zucchini. This mixture, including baby milk, makes a creamy combination for your baby to enjoy. Add a little boiled onion or leek for flavor.

Trim and thinly slice 1 small zucchini and place it in a saucepan. Cover the zucchini with boiling water, cover, and simmer for 5–10 minutes, or until tender. Drain well, reserving some of the cooking liquid. Purée in a blender or baby food mill with a little cooking liquid (if needed) until smooth. Place 2 tbsp. (30 ml) baby rice in a bowl. Add about 5 tbsp. (75 ml) warm baby milk and stir to make a smooth consistency. Add the zucchini purée and mix thoroughly. Adjust the consistency of the mixture by adding a little more baby milk, if necessary.

Useful Notes

❀: Yes   ❀: Yes

MASHED CAULIFLOWER AND BABY RICE

Makes about 12 tablespoons

Baby rice is easy to prepare and can be mixed with any fruit or vegetables. It thickens purées and adds extra energy (calories) for hungry babies.

Boil a generous 1 cup (250 ml) small cauliflower flowerets in a saucepan of boiling water for 5–10 minutes, or until cooked and tender. Drain well, reserving some of the cooking liquid. Measure 1 tbsp. (15 ml) baby rice into a bowl. Add 3 tbsp. (45 ml) of the reserved cooking liquid. Stir until the consistency is smooth. Mash or blend the cooked cauliflower until smooth and stir into the rice, mixing well. Adjust the consistency by adding more cooking liquid, or baby milk, if liked.

Useful Notes

❀: Yes   ❀: Yes

SWEET POTATO AND MUSHROOM PURÉE

Makes about 17 tablespoons

The delicious flavor of sweet potato makes a change from a plain, white potato, and combines well with mushrooms in this recipe. Baked sweet potato flesh can also be used.

Peel and dice 1 medium sweet potato. Place in a saucepan and cover with boiling water. Cover and simmer for 10–15 minutes, or until cooked and tender. Add 1½ cups (375 ml) sliced mushrooms 5 minutes before the end of the cooking time. Drain well, then put the cooked vegetables into a blender and purée with a little baby milk until smooth, or purée in a baby food mill. Spoon the mixture into a bowl and add enough baby milk (expressed breast milk or infant formula) to make the mixture the desired consistency.

Useful Notes

❄: Yes ❄: Yes

TURNIP AND CARROT PURÉE

Makes about 15 tablespoons

Substitute rutabaga or parsnip for the turnip in this recipe for a flavor variation. The sweetness of carrots makes them a popular vegetable with babies, and they are a good source of a type of vitamin A.
Add a little boiled onion or leek for extra flavor.

Peel and dice 1 small turnip and 1 small carrot. Place in a saucepan and cover with boiling water. Cover and simmer for 10–15 minutes, or until cooked and tender. Drain well, then purée or blend in a baby food mill with enough baby milk to make a smooth purée of the desired consistency.

Useful Notes

❄: Yes ❄: Yes

24

BROCCOLI AND POTATO PURÉE

Makes about 20 tablespoons

The deep green color of broccoli combined with potato makes this dish both look and taste good. Mixing stronger flavored vegetables, such as broccoli, with potato or baby rice is an excellent way of introducing new flavors and textures to your baby's mealtimes.

Peel and dice 1 medium potato. Place in a saucepan and cover with boiling water. Cover and simmer for 10 minutes, then add a generous ¹/₂ cup (125 ml) small broccoli flowerets. Return to a boil and simmer for 5–10 minutes longer, or until the vegetables are cooked and tender. Drain well, reserving some of the cooking liquid. Purée or blend in a baby food mill with enough cooking liquid to make a smooth purée of the desired consistency. Add a little baby milk instead of some of the cooking liquid, to give the mixture extra creaminess.

Useful Notes

❀: *Yes* ❀: *Yes*

VEGETABLE TRIO

Makes about 14 tablespoons

You can use any combination of three vegetables for this recipe. There are many delicious vegetables available, and the combination of two or three types makes a flavorful meal. Chilled, fresh, and frozen vegetable mixes are also sold, and can be used in this recipe. Just make sure the vegetables are well cooked and tender before puréeing.

Wash and thinly slice 1 small leek (use the white flesh only). Place in a saucepan and cover with boiling water. Cover and simmer for 10 minutes. Add 1¹/₂ cups (375 ml) sliced mushrooms and 1 small zucchini, thinly sliced. Cover and simmer for a 5–10 minutes longer, or until the vegetables are cooked and tender. Drain well, then purée or blend in a baby food mill with enough baby milk to make a smooth purée of the desired consistency.

Useful Notes

❀: *Yes* ❀: *Yes*

MASHED POTATO WITH GREENS

Makes about 20 tablespoons

Potatoes provide a good base for many vegetable mixtures, and help disguise the flavor of stronger-flavored foods, such as greens or Brussels sprouts, making them more appealing.

Peel and dice 1 medium potato. Place in a saucepan and cover with boiling water. Cover and simmer for 10 minutes. Add 1 cup (250 ml) shredded or chopped greens, cabbage, or Brussels sprouts and simmer for a 5–10 minutes longer, or until cooked and tender. Drain well, then purée or blend in a baby food mill with enough boiling water or baby milk to make a smooth purée.

Useful Notes

❀: Yes   ❋: Yes

CARROT AND CAULIFLOWER PURÉE

Makes about 13 tablespoons

Combining two differently textured vegetables works well in this recipe, with the carrot adding extra flavor and color.

Peel and thinly slice 1 medium carrot. Place in a saucepan and cover with boiling water. Cover and simmer for 10 minutes. Add ³/₄ cup (180 ml) small cauliflower flowerets. Simmer for 5–10 minutes longer, or until cooked and tender. Drain well, then purée or blend in a baby food mill, adding enough baby milk to make a smooth purée of the desired consistency.

Useful Notes

❀: Yes   ❋: Yes

26

PEA AND POTATO PURÉE

Makes about 22 tablespoons

Boiled potatoes work just as well in this recipe in place of the baked potato. You can also use frozen peas or beans instead of fresh.

Scrub 1 medium potato and bake in a preheated oven at 400°F (200°C) for about 1 hour, or until cooked and tender. Meanwhile, cook a scant ½ cup (125 ml) peas in a saucepan of boiling water for 5–10 minutes, or until cooked and tender. Drain well, reserving some of the cooking liquid. Remove the potato flesh from the skin. Purée or blend the potato flesh and peas in a baby food mill with enough cooking liquid or baby milk to make a smooth purée of the desired consistency. Use a sweet potato in place of the plain, white potato for extra flavor.

Nutrition Notes
Vitamin C: ▲

Useful Notes
✿: Yes   ❉: Yes

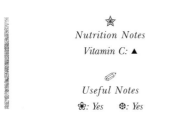

GREEN VEGETABLE PURÉE

Makes about 15 tablespoons

Add some mashed potato or prepared baby rice to this purée to "dilute" the flavor a little, or offer it at the slightly older 5–6 month stage.

Place ¼ cup (60 ml) small broccoli flowerets in a saucepan. Add ¼ cup (60 ml) peas and 1 cup (250 ml) chopped fresh spinach. Cover with boiling water. Cover the pan and simmer for about 10 minutes, or until cooked and tender. Drain the vegetables thoroughly, then purée or blend in a baby food mill with enough boiling water to make a smooth purée of the desired consistency.

Useful Notes
✿: Yes   ❉: Yes

27

BABY RICE AND BUTTER BEANS

Makes about 12 tablespoons

Beans are a useful source of protein, fiber, and iron for babies at this stage. Stores stock a wide variety of canned cooked legumes, and we have chosen butter beans for this recipe. These are particularly popular in the South, and you may have to look for them in health-food stores. Otherwise, substitute cannellini beans.

Rinse canned legumes well to remove the salt water. Some beans, such as red kidney beans, have tough skins which can be more difficult for a young baby to digest, so do not serve these for a few more weeks.

Place a generous ¹/₂ cup (125 ml) well rinsed and drained canned butter beans in a saucepan with a little boiling water. Cover the pan and simmer for about 5 minutes, or until piping hot. Drain well and purée or blend in a baby food mill with a little baby milk or boiling water to make a smooth purée. Place 1 tbsp. (15 ml) baby rice in a bowl and add 3 tbsp. (45 ml) boiling water or baby milk (expressed breast milk or infant formula). Stir in the bean purée, and mix well, adding a little extra baby water or milk to make the desired consistency.

Useful Notes

❋: Yes   ❋: Yes

28

MASHED CARROTS WITH PEAS AND BABY RICE

Makes about 12 tablespoons

Peas contain more protein, fiber, and iron than many other vegetables, so are good to include in a variety of dishes, especially when weaning is established (5–6 months).

Peel and thinly slice 1 small carrot. Place in a saucepan and cover with boiling water. Cover and simmer for 10 minutes. Add ¼ cup (60 ml) peas and simmer for 5–10 minutes longer until cooked and tender. Drain, reserving the cooking liquid. Place 1 tbsp. (15 ml) baby rice in a bowl and stir in 3 tbsp. (45 ml) of the reserved liquid to make a smooth consistency. Purée or blend the vegetables in a baby food mill with a little cooking liquid until smooth. Add to the baby rice and mix well, adding a little extra cooking liquid to make the desired consistency.

Useful Notes

✿: Yes   ✿: Yes

GREEN BEAN, ZUCCHINI, AND CHEESE PURÉE

Makes about 14 tablespoons

The addition of a little cheddar cheese to this recipe makes a flavorful and nutritious meal for your baby—cheese is an excellent source of protein and calcium. In this recipe, we use just a small amount of mild, full-fat hard cheese as an introduction to the flavor. You can add grated cheese to a number of vegetable dishes (it's especially good with cauliflower and mashed potato) to increase the nutritional value of the dish.

Trim and chop ¾ cup (375 ml) fresh green beans (or use frozen beans). Place them in a saucepan. Cover with boiling water, then cover and simmer for 5 minutes. Add 1 thinly sliced small zucchini, and simmer for a 5–10 minutes longer, or until cooked and tender. Drain well, reserving some of the cooking liquid. Purée or blend in a baby food mill with a little cooking liquid until smooth.

Add 1 tbsp. (15 ml) finely grated cheddar cheese and a little cooking liquid to make the purée the desired consistency.

Nutrition Notes
Calcium: ▲

Useful Notes
✿: Yes   ✿: Yes

GROUND BEEF WITH CARROT AND POTATO

Makes about 22 tablespoons

When your baby is accustomed to a variety of flavors and textures, start to introduce a wider range of foods. Meat is particularly useful, especially red meat, because it is an excellent source of a number of nutrients, including iron. You may find it useful to cook a batch of ground beef and freeze it in ice-cube trays, ready to combine with a variety of vegetables and potatoes.

Place 4 oz. (115 g) lean ground beef in a saucepan with 8 tbsp. (120 ml) beef stock (see page 14) or water and 1 small carrot, diced. Cover, bring to a boil, and simmer for 30–45 minutes, or until thoroughly cooked, stirring occasionally, adding a little extra stock or water if necessary. Peel and dice 1 small potato. Cook in a saucepan of boiling water for 10–15 minutes, or until cooked and tender. Drain thoroughly and mash. Cool the beef mixture slightly, then purée or blend in a baby food mill with the potato, adding a little boiling water, to make a smooth purée of the desired consistency. You can substitute baby rice for potato.

Nutrition Notes
Iron: ▲▲   Vitamin C: ▲

Useful Notes
❄: No   ❀: Yes

MIXED VEGETABLES WITH LENTILS

Makes about 18 tablespoons

As with peas and beans, lentils are a good source of protein, fiber, and iron. The texture of lentils works very well combined with any number of vegetables. Red, brown, or green lentils are all suitable for this recipe.

Place a generous ⅓ cup (85 ml) lentils in a saucepan and cover with plenty of boiling water. Cover and simmer for 20–30 minutes, or until cooked and tender. Drain well. Meanwhile, cook ⅔ cup (60 ml) diced mixed vegetables in a saucepan of boiling water for 10–15 minutes, or until tender. Drain well, reserving some of the cooking liquid. Purée or blend the lentils and vegetables in a baby food mill, adding enough cooking liquid to make the desired consistency.

Nutrition Notes
Iron: ▲   Vitamin C: ▲

Useful Notes
❄: Yes   ❀: Yes

CHICK-PEAS WITH AVOCADO

Makes about 4 tablespoons

This nutritious combination of chick-peas and avocado is a flavorful way of introducing beans and legumes into your baby's diet. Chick-peas are a good source of protein, fiber, vitamins, and minerals, and avocado is rich in vitamin E.

Drain and rinse 2 tbsp. (30 ml) canned chick-peas. Peel and mash 1 oz. (25 g) ripe avocado. Purée or blend the chick-peas and avocado in a baby food mill, adding enough boiling water or baby milk to make the desired consistency.

Useful Notes

❀: Yes ❀: No

MIXED VEGETABLES WITH CHEESE

Makes about 12 tablespoons

Use a selection of fresh vegetables in this recipe—try peas, carrots, and rutabaga, or broccoli, cauliflower, and carrots. Alternatively, use frozen vegetables—they work just as well and save preparation time.

Cook ¾ cup (375 ml) diced vegetables in a saucepan of boiling water for about 10–15 minutes until tender. Drain, then blend with a little boiling water to a smooth purée. Add 2 tbsp. (30 ml) finely grated cheddar cheese with enough baby milk to make the desired consistency.

☆

Nutrition Notes

Calcium: ▲▲   Vitamin C: ▲▲

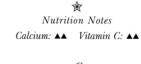

Useful Notes

❀: Yes ❀: Yes

MASHED PEARS WITH PEACHES

Makes about 17 tablespoons

Include some fresh fruit in your baby's diet every day to provide essential vitamins, especially vitamin C. With so many varieties available, there is plenty of choice—go for fresh fruit in season. Canned fruit in fruit juice, however, is good for a change, especially during winter.

Peel, core, and chop 1 ripe pear, and peel, pit, and chop 1 ripe peach. Blend or purée the fruit together, adding a little boiled water to make a smooth purée of the desired consistency. If the fruit is a little underripe, cook the prepared fruit first in a little boiling water until soft and tender, then purée. To make a more substantial dessert, add a little baby rice mixed with baby milk to the fruit.

☆
Nutrition Notes
Vitamin C: ▲▲

✎
Useful Notes
❀: Yes ❀: Yes

BANANA AND APRICOT PURÉE

Makes about 4 tablespoons

Bananas are the perfect weaning food. They are naturally sweet and easy to prepare, and have a smooth consistency when well mashed (there's no need to purée). Choose ripe bananas (the skin should be slightly speckled) which will be easy for your baby to digest. Bananas combined with apricots are simply delicious —and for adults, too!

Blanch 1 large or 2 small fresh ripe apricots in a saucepan of boiling water for 1–2 minutes. Drain the apricots, cool under running water, then peel and discard the skins. Halve and pit the apricots and chop the flesh. Purée or blend the apricot flesh and 1/3 of a small peeled banana together, adding a little baby milk to make a smooth, creamy purée of the desired consistency.

☆
Nutrition Notes
Vitamin C: ▲▲

✎
Useful Notes
❀: Yes ❀: No

STEWED APPLES AND PEARS

Makes about 11 tablespoons

Stewed apples are always a popular choice with babies and young children, and are easy to digest. Use eating apples which are naturally sweet, rather than cooking apples. In this recipe, we have combined fresh and canned fruit to make a delicious fruity mixture. Baked apple flesh works just as well.

Peel, core, and thinly slice 1 eating apple. Place in a saucepan with 2 tbsp. (30 ml) boiling water. Cover and simmer for about 5 minutes, or until cooked and pulpy. Meanwhile, chop 2 pear halves, packed in natural juice. Purée or blend the apple and pear together in a baby food mill, adding a little pear juice to make a smooth purée of the desired consistency.

Useful Notes

❀: Yes ❄: Yes

APRICOT AND PEAR PURÉE

Makes about 11 tablespoons

Canned fruits in natural juice are a quick, easy, and nutritious way of introducing fruit into your baby's diet. Many varieties are available, but make sure you choose a fruit packed in juice rather than in syrup. Try different combinations of fruits for variety.

Drain 4 canned apricot halves and 3 canned pear halves. Purée or blend the apricots and pears together in a baby food mill, adding a little of the canned fruit juice to make a smooth purée of the desired consistency. To give your baby extra calories and nutrients as well as a richer, creamier flavor, serve the fruit purée with a small quantity of baby rice or whole-milk plain yogurt.

Useful Notes

❀: Yes ❄: Yes

33

FRUIT COCKTAIL PURÉE

Makes about 12 tablespoons

Combinations of canned fruit are easy to prepare, and the whole family can enjoy this dish. Simply remove a small quantity to purée for your baby. Use your own combination of fruits or use a can of fruit cocktail or fruit salad as an alternative.

Purée or blend 2 canned pear halves, 6 canned peach slices, 2 canned apricot halves, and 12 canned mandarins together, adding enough fruit juice or boiled water to make a smooth purée of the desired consistency.

Useful Notes

❀: *Yes*   ❀: *Yes*

BABY RICE AND NECTARINE PURÉE

Makes about 11 tablespoons

Fresh nectarines are a delicious fruit for your baby to enjoy. Choose ripe, juicy fruits for this tasty recipe.

Place 2 tbsp. (30 ml) baby rice in a bowl. Add 5 tbsp. (75 ml) warm, previously boiled water and mix to a smooth consistency. Peel, pit, and chop 1 fresh nectarine, then purée or blend in a baby food mill with a little boiled water to make a smooth purée. Add the puréed nectarine to the baby rice and mix thoroughly, adding a little extra boiled water to make the desired consistency.

Nutrition Notes

Vitamin C: ▲▲

Useful Notes

❀: *Yes*   ❀: *Yes*

STRAWBERRY AND APPLE PURÉE

Makes about 12 tablespoons

When your baby is used to the flavor of fruits, such as pears, apples, and bananas, start introducing a wider variety of fruits. If there is a history of allergies in your family, wait until your baby is more than 6 months before introducing soft summer fruits such as strawberries. In this recipe, strawberries and stewed apple make a colorful combination. Choose a sweet variety of eating apple, such as Red Delicious. Press the mashed strawberries through a fine nylon strainer to remove as many seeds as possible.

Peel, core, and thinly slice 1 eating apple. Place in a saucepan with 2 tbsp. (30 ml) boiling water. Cover and simmer for about 5 minutes, or until cooked and pulpy. Meanwhile, purée or blend ¾ cup (375 ml) ripe strawberries in a baby food mill. Press through a fine, nylon strainer to remove as many seeds as possible. Discard any seeds. Mix together the apple pulp and strawberries and blend with a little boiled water to make a smooth purée of the desired consistency.

Nutrition Notes

Vitamin C: ▲▲

Useful Notes

❄: Yes   ❄: Yes

MASHED BANANA WITH BABY RICE

Makes about 5 tablespoons

In this recipe, baby rice combines well with banana to make a substantial dessert.

Place 1 tbsp. (15 ml) baby rice in a bowl. Add 3 tbsp. (45 ml) warm baby milk and mix to a smooth consistency. Mash 2 oz. (55 g) ripe peeled banana. Add to the rice and mix well, adding a little extra baby milk to make the desired consistency.

Useful Notes

❄: Yes   ❄: No

MANGO AND APRICOT PURÉE

Makes about 14 tablespoons

Fresh mangoes are a good source of vitamin C and have a pleasant texture. Combined with apricots, this recipe is colorful and packed full of nutrients.

Peel, seed, and chop 1 small fresh ripe mango. Purée or blend the mango and 4 apricot halves packed in natural juice in a baby food mill with a little apricot juice or boiled water, to make a smooth purée of the desired consistency.

Nutrition Notes
Vitamin C: ▲▲

Useful Notes
❋: *Yes* ❋: *Yes*

MELON WITH PEACHES

Makes about 10 tablespoons

Melon is a refreshing fruit and ideal served on its own or combined with other fruits, such as peaches. For the best flavor, choose a ripe melon. Galia is fragrant with a medium-sweet taste.

Peel, pit, and chop 1 fresh peach. Peel, seed, and chop 4 oz. (115 g) melon. Purée or blend the peach and melon together to form a smooth purée. Add a little boiled water to make the desired consistency, if necessary.

Nutrition Notes
Vitamin C: ▲▲

Useful Notes
❋: *Yes* ❋: *Yes*

PLUMS WITH BANANA

Makes about 4 tablespoons)

Fresh or canned plums may be used for this recipe. We have suggested canned plums for speed and convenience. Fresh plums should be peeled, pitted, and stewed before using.

Purée or blend ¹/₂ of a small peeled banana and 2 peeled and pitted canned plums together, adding a little plum juice or baby milk to make a smooth purée of the desired consistency.

Useful Notes

❀: Yes ❀: No

AVOCADO AND MELON PURÉE

Makes about 4 tablespoons

Avocado is one of the only fruits which contains vitamin E. The flesh has a rich flavor, but combined with a more watery fruit, such as melon in this recipe, it becomes much lighter.

Peel and mash 1 oz. (25 g) ripe avocado and peel, seed, and chop 1 oz. (25 g) melon. Purée or blend the avocado and melon together, adding enough boiled water or baby milk to make a smooth purée of the desired consistency. For variety, try a combination of puréed avocado and mashed ripe banana. This is an equally delicious combination.

Useful Notes

❀: Yes ❀: No

37

tHe secoND staGe

By the time your baby is 6 months old, weaning should be well established. Using the recipes presented in Chapter 1, your baby will already be enjoying a variety of tastes and textures from a range of different foods. During the second stage—the 6-9 month period—your baby and her attitude toward food will develop rapidly. She will be ready for stronger flavors and foods with interesting and more challenging textures. The following pages detail the range of foods and drinks to introduce into your baby's diet at this stage, and the vitamins and minerals found in various foods which are vital to her growing needs.

DEVELOPING EATING HABITS

The main factor to bear in mind at this stage is that your baby's growth is likely to occur in spurts, so you may notice her appetite changing from day to day, sometimes wanting more, sometimes less food. Be sensitive to this, and don't force her to eat if she suddenly wants or eats less food than usual. Remember, a healthy baby won't go hungry!

At around 6 months, when your baby is able to sit up reasonably well, you will probably have her sitting in a high chair for feeding. By 7 months, she may have cut her first teeth. At this stage, babies can start to enjoy finger foods, which help to develop chewing. Gradually offering foods which are mashed and chopped, rather than puréed, also helps her to learn to chew, so that by the end of her first year she will be able to enjoy a whole range of family foods, just chopped up. It's important to positively encourage chewing at this stage, because some babies can become lazy, preferring to drink all their calories from milk, rather than eat solid food.

Never leave your baby alone when feeding, especially when she is eating finger foods or dishes with small pieces of food in it. Offer small amounts at a time so that she gets used to different textured food, and give her time to chew and swallow each mouthful before offering more.

Foods to include now

From 6 months onward, food becomes more important as a source of nutrition for your baby, although she should still be having about 2½ cups (625 ml) of milk a day, either as a drink or in foods, or probably both. Try to offer food first at mealtimes, and then milk afterward, or as a drink in between meals (see page 41 for suitable milks).

You can start to increase the types of food offered now, including a wider variety of protein foods, such as different meats, poultry, beans, and legumes, fish, liver, and egg. Try mixing foods together more, such as combining vegetables with meat and potatoes, or cheese with vegetables and fish (see our recipe suggestions for delicious combinations). Foods containing gluten can also be introduced now, widening the choice of foods offered. Look at the checklist below, to see which foods are suitable.

Starchy foods: Wheat cereals (such as wheat bisks mashed with milk), oats (such as oatmeal), rice, potatoes, pasta, and bread (avoid mixed-grain or whole-grain types). Try introducing some whole-wheat varieties.
Offer 2–3 servings daily.

Vegetables and fruits: Increase the variety: citrus fruits, tomatoes, and raw soft fruit. Many can be offered as finger foods, such as cooked vegetables. Babies do not need a dessert, and it is preferable to use fruit to satisfy a sweet tooth.
Offer 2 or more servings daily.

Meat and meat alternatives: Well-cooked meats, fish (especially white fish), and beans and legumes, all to be ground or puréed. Hard-cooked whole egg is suitable but best left to nearer 9 months.
Offer one serving of foods from this group daily.

Milk and dairy products: About 2¼–2½ cups (560–625 ml) breast milk or infant formula should be drunk daily (see page 41 for a guide to milk and drinks). Milk, including whole cows' milk, can also be used to mix with solids. Other dairy products, such as whole-milk yogurt, cheese, and milk-based sauces, such as custards or milk puddings, can be eaten as well as, or instead of, some of the milk as a drink.

Foods to avoid at this stage include whole nuts (finely ground nut pastes, like peanut butter, are fine), salt, and hot spices. Other herbs and spices can now be introduced gradually, allowing your baby to become accustomed to more "adult" flavors.

If there is a history of allergies in your family, introduce one new food at a time to start with, combined with foods you know your baby can tolerate. For example, try chicken with mashed potato and carrots or peas one day, and introduce oatmeal for breakfast on another day, and so on, until you are happy that your baby does not have any adverse reactions to different foods. Leave approximately 48 hours between introducing new foods, to allow any delayed reaction to occur.

Citrus fruits, tomatoes, and egg white, can be particularly allergenic. If you are worried about allergies, avoid these foods until your baby is around 7–8 months. If she does react to certain foods, ask your pediatrician for advice.

Iron and other minerals and vitamins

For the first six months of life, your baby should have a good store of iron in her body, providing you have eaten a well-balanced diet during pregnancy. After this time, however, dietary sources of iron become more important, because the amount in breast milk, in particular, is not enough to meet growing needs. A lack of iron has been shown to slow down a baby's growth and development, and can cause loss of appetite, general tiredness, and apathy.

Good dietary sources of iron include red meat and other meats such as chicken, some vegetables and fortified cereals, and infant formula. The iron in meat is more easily absorbed than that found in vegetable and cereal foods, so it is a good idea to introduce some of these foods when your baby is 6–8 months old. Look for those recipes in this chapter which are a useful or a rich source of iron.

The absorption of iron and other minerals, such as zinc, from cereal and vegetable sources is enhanced by vitamin C, so including fruits and vegetables rich in this vitamin in the diet will help the uptake of iron from nonmeat sources. Once again, check the recipes to see which are high in vitamin C.

Vitamins

If breast milk continues to be the main drink for your baby after six months, your pediatrician may prescribe supplements, depending on your baby's overall diet. Babies drinking at least 2½ cups (625 ml) of infant formula each day do not need supplements until a year old. Vitamin A and D supplements are recommended for all 1–5 year olds. If in doubt, ask your pediatrician for advice.

Finger foods

Suitable finger foods are a great way for your baby to discover a variety of different tastes and textures of food, and is a preliminary to self-feeding. Try any of the following, and remember to stay close by while she sucks and chews on the food pieces, in case she chokes.

- toast or bread fingers (encourage whole-wheat); breadsticks
- rusks (reduced-sugar varieties)
- cooked vegetables, such as green beans, carrot sticks, cubes of potato, and tomato slices (peeled and seeded)
- soft-textured, ripe fruit, such as banana, slices of avocado, kiwi fruit, mango, sliced strawberries, melon, and segments of seeded tangerines
- slices of peeled and cored apple, peeled and cored pear, and peeled peach
- cubes of hard cheese (cheddar-type) or grated cheese
- chopped hard-cooked egg
- dry, oat-based ring-shaped pieces of cereal, which are also good for hand-eye coordination

Drinks

The best drinks at this stage are milk and water. Very diluted fruit juices and baby herbal drinks can also be given, but only at mealtimes—even very dilute fruit juice can be potentially damaging to teeth. Try to accustom your baby to drinking water or milk between meals, rather than diluted juices. It's also a good time to offer some drinks from a training cup. This will take getting used to, but if offered regularly (with every meal), your baby will soon learn to drink from the cup.

Suitable milks for 6–12-month-old babies

Breast milk and infant formula are suitable as a main drink. Whole cows' milk can be used from now on in cooking, but is not suitable as a main drink until your baby is over one year old because it is low in iron. Skim or low-fat milks should not be drunk at this stage.

BEEF AND VEGETABLE CASSEROLE

Makes about 31 tablespoons ❋ *PREPARATION TIME:* 15 minutes ❋ *COOKING TIME:* 1–1½ hours

An easy casserole to make and a good way of introducing tomatoes into your baby's diet. The combination of beef and fresh vegetables makes this a flavorful and nutritious meal. Add some mashed potato to complete the meal before serving.

½ lb (225 g) lean ground beef

1 cup (250 ml) canned chopped tomatoes

1 carrot, finely chopped

1 small onion, finely chopped

1 cup (250 ml) finely chopped mushrooms

1 celery stalk, finely chopped

1 tbsp. (15 ml) tomato ketchup

½ cup (125 ml) vegetable stock (see page 14) or water

pinch of dried Italian seasoning

1 Place the ground beef in a flameproof, ovenproof casserole dish and cook gently until browned all over.

2 Strain the chopped tomatoes, discarding the seeds. Add the tomato pulp and juice to the casserole. Add all the remaining ingredients to the dish and stir thoroughly to mix.

3 Cover the casserole dish and bake in a preheated oven at 350°F (180°C) for 1–1½ hours, or until the beef and vegetables are cooked through and very tender, stirring occasionally.

4 Remove the dish from the oven. Mash or purée the casserole, adding a small quantity of extra stock if needed, to make the desired consistency.

Variations

Use ground pork, chicken, or turkey in place of the beef.

❋

Cook's Tips

Recipe can easily be adapted for an adult meal. This casserole will serve 1 adult and 1 baby. Serve the adult portion with mashed potatoes or boiled new potatoes.

Nutrition Notes

Vitamin C: ▲

Useful Notes

❀: No ❋: Yes

CHEESY COD AND ZUCCHINI SUPPER

Makes about 20 tablespoons ❋ *PREPARATION TIME:* 10 minutes ❋ *COOKING TIME:* 20 minutes

White fish is a good source of protein, and can now be introduced into your baby's diet. It has a good, flaky texture which is easy to eat. Serve with fingers of toast to complete the nutritional balance of the dish.

4 oz. (115 g) skinless, boneless cod fillet

1 small zucchini, thinly sliced

1 bay leaf

⅔ cup (160 ml) milk

1 tbsp. (15 ml) butter or margarine

1 tbsp. (15 ml) all-purpose flour

⅓ cup (80 ml) finely grated cheddar cheese

2 tsp. (10 ml) chopped fresh parsley

1 Place the cod, zucchini, and bay leaf in a skillet. Pour the milk over, then cover the pan. Bring the milk slowly to a boil and simmer gently for about 15 minutes, or until the fish flakes and zucchini are cooked and tender.

2 Using a slotted spoon, carefully remove the fish and zucchini from the milk. Place on a warmed plate, cover, and keep warm. Remove and discard the bay leaf.

3 Place the milk in a saucepan with the butter or margarine and flour. Heat gently, whisking continuously, until the sauce comes to a boil and thickens. Simmer gently for 2 minutes, stirring.

4 Remove the pan from the heat and stir in the cheese and parsley. Flake the fish and add to the sauce with the zucchini, mixing well. Mash or purée, adding a little extra milk if needed.

Variations

Use other white fish, such as flounder or haddock, in place of the cod.

Use 1$\frac{1}{2}$ cups (375 ml) sliced mushrooms in place of the zucchini.

Use Colby cheese in place of the cheddar cheese.

Cook's Tips

Remember with any type of fish, all the small bones must be removed and discarded before feeding it to your baby.

Recipe can easily be adapted for an adult meal. This recipe will serve 1 adult and 1 baby. Serve the adult portion with a mixture of cooked fresh vegetables.

Nutrition Notes

Calcium: ▲

Useful Notes

❂: No   ❂: Yes

43

SUMMER VEGETABLE MEDLEY

Makes about 27 tablespoons
PREPARATION TIME: 15 minutes
COOKING TIME: 8-10 minutes

An excellent way of introducing a variety of vegetables into your baby's diet, this appetizing stir-fry is full of nutrients, too. Vary the mixture of vegetables used depending on what you already have in the refrigerator, or choose vegetables in season.

$^1/_4$ cup (60 ml) pasta shapes, such as twists or tubes

1 tbsp. (15 ml) butter or margarine

1 tbsp. (15 ml) all-purpose plain flour

1 cup (250 ml) vegetable stock (see page 14), cooled, or water

2 tsp. (10 ml) sunflower oil

2 shallots, finely chopped

1 small carrot, finely chopped

1 small zucchini, finely chopped

4 baby corn cobs, thinly sliced

2 oz. (55 g) skinned and finely chopped, seeded red pepper

$^1/_3$ cup (80 ml) thinly sliced mushrooms

1 tbsp. (15 ml) chopped fresh basil

1 Cook the pasta in a saucepan of boiling unsalted water for about 12 minutes, until cooked and tender.

2 Meanwhile, place the butter or margarine, flour, and stock or water in a saucepan. Heat gently, whisking, until the sauce comes to a boil and thickens.

Simmer gently for 2 minutes, stirring. Remove from the heat and set aside.

3 Heat the oil in a nonstick skillet or wok. Add the prepared shallots, carrot, zucchini, baby corn, red pepper, and mushrooms. Stir-fry over medium heat for approximately 8–10 minutes, or until all the vegetables in the pan are well cooked and very tender.

4 Drain the pasta and add to the vegetables with the sauce and chopped fresh basil. Stir thoroughly to mix, then mash or purée, adding a little extra stock if needed, to make the desired consistency.

Variations

Use whole-wheat pasta or rice in place of the white pasta.

Use canned or frozen baby corn cobs if fresh are not available.

Use 2 oz. (55 g) small broccoli or cauliflower flowerets in place of the zucchini.

Cook's Tips

Remember when stir-frying vegetables for a baby or young child to cook the vegetables until they are soft rather than crisp, to make them easier to mash or purée and digest.

Recipe can easily be adapted for an adult meal. This medley will serve 1 adult and 1 baby. Serve the adult portion with some warmed crusty bread.

Nutrition Notes

Vitamin C: ▲▲

Useful Notes

❀: *Yes*   ✲: *Yes*

PASTA WITH TUNA, SPINACH, AND CREAM CHEESE

Makes about 8 tablespoons ✪ *PREPARATION TIME:* 5 minutes ✪ *COOKING TIME:* 12 minutes

Pasta is an excellent source of starchy carbohydrate and has an interesting texture which is often a favorite with babies. We have used whole-wheat pasta in this recipe, but white pasta will work just as well.

¹/₄ cup (60 ml) whole-wheat pasta shapes, such as shells or twists

1 oz. (25 g) fresh spinach

2 tbsp. (30 ml) canned tuna (in water or oil), drained and flaked

¹/₄ cup (60 ml) light cream cheese

pinch of dried tarragon (optional)

1 Cook the pasta in a saucepan of boiling water for about 12 minutes, or until cooked and tender.

2 Meanwhile, thoroughly wash the spinach and shred the leaves. Cook in a saucepan with a little boiling water for 2–3 minutes, or until cooked and tender.

3 Drain well and press out any excess water using the back of a wooden spoon or a potato masher. Chop the spinach finely and set aside.

4 Mash the tuna, then add the cream cheese and dried tarragon, if using, and mix until thoroughly blended.

5 Drain the pasta and place it in a bowl. Add the cooked spinach and tuna mixture and stir to mix.

6 Mash or purée, adding a little boiled water or milk if needed, to make the desired consistency.

Variations

Use other canned fish, such as salmon, in place of the tuna.

Use spring greens, cabbage, or broccoli in place of the spinach.

Cook's Tips

Remember to choose fish canned in water or oil, rather than in brine (salt water). The salt content of fish canned in brine is too high for your baby's system.

Useful Notes

❀: *No*   ✲: *No*

CREAMY LENTIL HOTPOT

Makes about 34 tablespoons ✿ *PREPARATION TIME:* 10 minutes ✿ *COOKING TIME:* 1–1½ hours

Lentils are a good source of protein, fiber, and iron. This mixture of lentils, vegetables, and yogurt makes a delicious, nutritious combination.

generous ⅓ cup (85 ml) green lentils

2 cups (500 ml) vegetable stock (see page 14) or water

1 small onion, finely chopped

1 small carrot, finely chopped

1 small turnip, diced

1 celery stalk, finely chopped

1 cup (250 ml) canned chopped tomatoes

1 tbsp. (15 ml) chopped fresh parsley

2 tbsp. (30 ml) whole-milk plain yogurt

1 Place the lentils, stock, onion, carrot, turnip, and celery in an ovenproof dish and stir to mix.

2 Strain the tomatoes and discard the seeds. Add the tomato pulp and juice to the lentil mixture and mix well.

3 Cover and cook in a preheated oven at 350°F (180°C) for 1–1½ hours, or until the lentils and vegetables are cooked and tender, stirring once or twice.

4 Stir in the parsley or mixed herbs and yogurt, then mash or purée, adding a little extra stock if needed, to make the desired consistency.

❧
Variations
Use brown or red lentils in place of the green.

✿

Cook's Tips
Bottled strained tomatoes or tomato juice can be used in place of the chopped tomatoes, but make sure neither contains salt.

Recipe can easily be adapted for an adult meal. This hotpot will serve 1 adult and 1 baby. Serve the adult portion with boiled brown rice or pasta.

☆

Nutrition Notes
Vitamin C: ▲

✐

Useful Notes
❀: Yes ❀: Yes

STIR-FRIED CHICKEN WITH AVOCADO AND RICE

Makes about 29 tablespoons ✿ *PREPARATION TIME:* 35 minutes ✿ *COOKING TIME:* 10 minutes

Stir-fries are full of delicious flavor and color. Remember when cooking stir-fries for babies and young children that the vegetables will need more cooking than for adults, and should be tender rather than crisp. Increase the ingredient quantities and all the family can enjoy this savory stir-fry together!

¼ cup (60 ml) long-grain brown rice

2 tsp. (10 ml) sunflower oil

1 small skinless, boneless chicken breast half, cut into thin strips

1 small leek, washed and thinly sliced

½ celery stalk, finely chopped

¾ cup (180 ml) sliced mushrooms

2 tbsp. (30 ml) chicken stock (see page 14) or water

2 tbsp. (30 ml) unsweetened apple juice

1 oz. (25 g) peeled avocado, finely chopped and tossed in a little lemon juice

1 Cook the rice in a saucepan of boiling water for about 35 minutes, until tender.

2 Meanwhile, heat the oil in a large, nonstick skillet or wok. Add the chicken strips and stir-fry over medium heat for about 2 minutes.

3 Add the leek, celery, and mushrooms to the pan and continue to stir-fry for a 5–7 minutes longer, or until the chicken

strips and all the vegetables are cooked and very tender.

4 Rinse and drain the rice. Add to the skillet or wok with the stock or water and apple juice. Stir-fry for about 2 minutes, until thoroughly heated.

5 Stir in the avocado, then mash or purée, adding a little extra stock if needed, to make the desired consistency.

Variations
Use white rice in place of the brown rice.
Use turkey in place of the chicken.
Use 1 small onion or 2 shallots in place of the leek.

❁
Cook's Tips
Once an avocado has been peeled and sliced or chopped, it should be added to a recipe immediately or tossed in lemon juice or acidulated water to prevent discoloration.

To freeze this recipe, do not add the avocado before freezing. Simply purée or mash the rice and chicken mixture and freeze. Once defrosted and reheated thoroughly, add the mashed avocado.

Recipe can easily be adapted for an adult meal. This stir-fry will serve 1 adult and 1 baby. Serve the adult portion with a thick slice of fresh crusty bread.

✎
Useful Notes
❀: No   ❁: Yes, but see above

47

HAM AND PEPPER SCRAMBLE

Makes about 4 tablespoons ❀ *PREPARATION TIME:* 10 minutes ❀ *COOKING TIME:* 3–4 minutes

Make sure that the egg is hard-cooked all the way through before serving. Add fingers of toast to serve to complete the meal. Hard-cooked whole egg is best introduced nearer to 9 months of age.

small knob of butter or margarine

2 tbsp. (30 ml) skinned and finely chopped seeded red pepper

1 egg

1 tbsp. (15 ml) milk

1 tbsp. (15 ml) finely chopped lean cooked ham

a little chopped fresh parsley

1 Melt the butter or margarine in a small saucepan. Add the pepper and cook gently for about 5 minutes, or until softened, stirring occasionally.

2 Lightly beat the egg and milk together and add to the pan. Cook gently, stirring continuously, until the mixture thickens and the egg is well cooked.

3 Remove the pan from the heat and stir in the ham and parsley, mixing well.

4 Mash or lightly purée, adding a little extra milk if needed, to make the desired consistency.

Variations

Use 1 shallot in place of the pepper.

Use cooked chicken or lean cooked beef in place of the ham.

❀

Cook's Tips

To skin a pepper, halve the pepper and place it cut-side down on the rack in a broiler pan. Place under a hot broiler for 10–15 minutes, until the skin is charred and blackened. Cover the pepper with a clean damp dish towel, or wrap in a piece of foil. Set aside to cool. Once cool, remove and discard the skin, core, and seeds from the pepper and prepare according to the recipe.

☆

Nutrition Notes

Vitamin C: ▲▲

✎

Useful Notes

 ❀: *No* ❀: *No*

BEAN AND VEGETABLE BAKE

Makes about 40 tablespoons ✪ *PREPARATION TIME:* 20 minutes ✪ *COOKING TIME:* 30 minutes

This delicious potato-topped dish is a flavorful way of serving nutritious beans and vegetables. This recipe makes quite a large number of baby servings. Alternatively, it makes enough to serve 2–3 adults and 1 baby to enjoy together as a family.

1 large potato, peeled and diced

a little milk and butter or margarine, to mix

1 small leek, washed and thinly sliced

1 tbsp. (15 ml) butter or margarine

1 tbsp. (15 ml) all-purpose flour

³/₄ cup (180 ml) milk

¹/₂ cup (125 g) finely grated cheddar cheese

²/₃ cup (160 ml) chopped button mushrooms

1¹/₄ cups (310 ml) canned red kidney beans, rinsed and drained

pinch of dried Herbes de Provence

Variations

Use prepared instant mashed potatoes instead of a fresh potato.

Use sweet potato in place of the standard potato.

Use Edam or Jarlsberg cheese in place of the cheddar cheese.

✪

Cook's Tips

The canned kidney beans in this recipe can also be used to make a bean salad. Simply rinse and drain the beans, toss them in a little oil-and-vinegar dressing, and serve with crusty bread.

Recipe can easily be adapted for an adult meal. This bake will serve 2–3 adults and 1 baby. Serve the adult portions with crusty bread and a mixed leaf salad.

☆

Nutrition Notes

Calcium: ▲

Useful Notes

❀: *Yes* ✿: *Yes*

1 Cook the potato in a saucepan of boiling water for about 15 minutes, until cooked and tender. Drain well, then mash thoroughly with a little milk and butter or margarine until smooth. Set aside.

2 Place the leek in a saucepan and cover with boiling water. Cover and simmer for 5 minutes. Drain and keep warm.

3 Meanwhile, place the butter or margarine, flour, and milk in a saucepan and heat gently, whisking continuously, until the sauce comes to a boil and thickens. Simmer gently for 2 minutes, stirring.

4 Remove the pan from the heat and add the cheese, stirring until it has melted. Add the leek and remaining ingredients and mix well.

5 Spoon the mixture into an ovenproof dish, then cover the top with the mashed potato. Mark the potato with a fork to create an all-over texture. Bake in a pre-heated oven at 400°F (200°C) for 30 minutes, or until lightly browned on top.

6 Mash or purée, adding a little extra stock or milk if needed, to make the desired consistency.

POTATO, LEEK, AND CHEESE PIE

Makes about 30 tablespoons ❁ *PREPARATION TIME:* 20 minutes ❁ *COOKING TIME:* 30 minutes

Potatoes are a versatile, filling food for everyone, including babies and young children, and this potato bake is a delicious way of serving them. Use one sweet potato and one standard potato for a change.

2 medium potatoes, peeled and diced

1 carrot, sliced

1 leek, washed and sliced

¾ cup (180 ml) finely grated cheddar cheese

1 tbsp. (15 ml) chopped fresh parsley

a little milk, to mix (optional)

1 Place the potatoes and carrot in a saucepan and cover with boiling water. Cover and simmer for 10 minutes, then add the leek.

2 Cover and cook for 5–10 minutes longer, or until the vegetables are cooked and tender.

3 Drain well, then mash thoroughly. Add the cheese, parsley, and a little milk, mixing well, until smooth.

4 Spoon into a lightly greased, shallow, ovenproof dish and bake in a preheated oven at 375°F (190°C) on the middle shelf for about 30 minutes, or until lightly browned on top.

5 Mash the pie, adding a small quantity of extra milk if needed, to make the food the desired consistency.

Variations

Use 4 scallions or 3 shallots in place of the leek.

Use 1 small parsnip in place of the carrot.

Use chopped fresh mixed herbs in place of the parsley.

Cook's Tips

When preparing leeks, it is important to remove all the soil and dirt that collects within their layers. Sliced leeks can simply be washed thoroughly under running water. Whole leeks should be split in half almost to the root and washed thoroughly in cold water to loosen any dirt.

Recipe can easily be adapted for an adult meal. This pie will serve 1 adult and 1 baby. Serve the adult portion with cooked fresh vegetables.

Nutrition Notes
Calcium: ▲▲   Vitamin C: ▲

Useful Notes
❁: Yes   ❁: Yes

MACARONI AND CHEESE WITH BROCCOLI

Makes about 26 tablespoons *PREPARATION TIME:* 15 minutes ❁ *COOKING TIME:* 20 minutes

The addition of broccoli and zucchini to this macaroni and cheese adds flavor and color. It's a good way of introducing broccoli to your child's diet. The other ingredients help disguise the strong flavor.

½ cup (125 ml) short-cut whole-wheat macaroni

¼ cup (60 ml) small broccoli flowerets

1 small zucchini, sliced

1 tbsp. (15 ml) butter or margarine

1 tbsp. (15 ml) all-purpose flour

about ¾ cup (180 ml) milk

½ cup (125 ml) finely grated cheddar cheese

1 Cook the macaroni in a saucepan of boiling water for about 10 minutes, or until just tender. Drain thoroughly, keep warm, and set aside.

2 Meanwhile, cook the broccoli and zucchini in a little boiling water for 5 minutes, or until cooked and tender. Drain well and keep warm.

3 Place the butter or margarine, flour, and milk in a saucepan and heat gently, whisking continuously, until the sauce comes to a boil and thickens. Simmer gently for 2 minutes, stirring.

4 Remove the pan from the heat and stir in the cheese. Add the macaroni and vegetables and mix well.

5 Spoon into an ovenproof dish and bake in a preheated oven 400°F (200°C) for about 20 minutes, until golden brown and bubbling on top.

6 Mash or purée, adding a little extra milk if needed, to make the food the desired consistency.

Variations
Use 1 leek in place of the zucchini.
Use Gruyère cheese in place of the cheddar cheese.
Use cauliflower in place of the broccoli.

Cook's Tips
Recipe can easily be adapted for an adult meal.

This recipe will serve 1 adult and 1 baby.
Serve the adult portion with a mixed side salad.

☆
Nutrition Notes
Calcium: ▲   Vitamin C: ▲

Useful Notes
❀: *Yes*   ❀: *Yes*

51

PLUM AND LEMON RICE DESSERT

Makes about 18 tablespoons ✿ *PREPARATION TIME: 45 minutes* ✿ *COOKING TIME: 20–30 minutes*

A flavorful and fruity alternative to rice pudding. You can stew other fruits, such as apples or pears, and use them in place of the plums for a change.

2 tbsp. (30 ml) white pudding rice

1¼ cups (310 ml) milk

2 large ripe plums

1 tbsp. (15 ml) sugar

knob of butter or margarine

½ tsp. (25 ml) finely grated lemon peel

1 Place the rice and milk in a heavy-based saucepan and bring gently to a boil over low heat.

2 Simmer for 30–45 minutes, or until the rice is tender and most of the milk has been absorbed, stirring occasionally.

3 Meanwhile, blanch the plums in a saucepan of boiling water for 1 minute. Drain and set aside to cool.

4 Skin and pit the plums, then mash or finely chop the plum flesh and mix with the sugar.

5 Spoon the mashed or chopped plums into the base of a lightly greased oven-proof dish. Stir the butter or margarine and the lemon peel into the rice mixture, then spoon the rice over the plums, spreading it evenly.

6 Bake in a preheated oven at 350°F (180°C) for 20–30 minutes, until lightly browned on top. Mash or purée, adding a little extra milk if needed, to make the desired consistency. Serve warm or chilled. Cover and keep in the refrigerator for up to 1 day.

Variations

Use other fruits, such as pears, peaches, or apricots, in place of the plums.

Use orange or lime peel or a little ground apple-pie spice or ginger in place of the lemon peel.

Use canned plums in place of the fresh plums. There is no need to blanch canned plums, but remember to remove and discard the skins and pits before mashing the fruit.

Cook's Tip

Recipe can be adapted for an adult meal. This dessert serves 1 adult and 1 baby. Serve the adult portion with extra fruit and ice cream or yogurt

Useful Notes
❀: *Yes* ❀: *Yes*

POACHED PLUM AND PEAR COMPOTE

Makes about 14 tablespoons ✤ *PREPARATION TIME:* 5 minutes ✤ *COOKING TIME:* 10–15 minutes

Poaching fruits is a delicious way to serve fresh fruit, and is especially good for babies because the fruit is very soft and palatable. Dried fruit adds natural sweetness so there is no need to add extra sugar.

3 ripe plums, peeled, halved, pitted, and chopped

¹/₂ cup (125 ml) finely chopped ready-to-eat dried pears

¹/₂ cup (125 ml) unsweetened apple juice

1 Place the plums, pears, and apple juice in a saucepan and stir to mix. Cover and bring to a boil. Simmer gently for 10–15 minutes, or until the plums are cooked and tender, stirring occasionally.

2 Remove the pan from the heat and leave the compote to cool slightly, then mash or purée the mixture in a blender or food processor to the desired consistency. Serve warm or chilled.

Variations
Use other fruits, such as peaches and apricots, in place of the plums.

Use other ready-to-eat dried fruit, such as apricots or peaches, in place of the pears.

Use unsweetened orange or pineapple juice in place of the apple juice.

Cook's Tips
An easy way to peel plums is to blanch whole fruits in boiling water for 1–2 minutes, cool slightly, and peel the skins off them.

Increase the quantities and use the poached plums as the basis for a fruit cobbler or fruit pie.

Recipe can easily be adapted for an adult meal.

This dessert will serve 1–2 adults and 1 baby. Serve the adult portion(s) with ice cream.

Cover and keep in the refrigerator for up to 1 day.

Useful Notes
❄: Yes ✤: Yes

STEWED APPLE WITH CINNAMON

Makes about 12 tablespoons ✤ *PREPARATION TIME:* 10 minutes ✤ *COOKING TIME:* 10–15 minutes

Stewed fruits are always a popular choice for babies, and are so quick and easy to prepare. The addition of a little ground cinnamon and finely chopped dates adds extra flavor and texture to this recipe. Serve with yogurt for a nutritious dessert.

2 eating apples

2 tbsp. (30 ml) unsweetened apple juice

pinch of ground cinnamon

2 tbsp. (30 ml) finely chopped dried dates

1 Peel, core, and slice the apples. Place them in a saucepan with the apple juice.

2 Cover and cook gently until the apples are soft and pulpy, stirring occasionally.

3 Remove the pan from the heat and mash the apple to form a smooth purée. Stir in the cinnamon and dates.

4 Serve warm or cold, and blend to the desired consistency before serving.

Variations
Add a little finely grated orange or lemon peel in place of the cinnamon.

Use 2 dessert pears in place of the apples.

Cook's Tips
A quick-and-easy way to chop dried fruit such as dates is to snip them into small pieces using a pair of clean kitchen scissors.

Recipe can easily be adapted for an adult meal. This dessert will serve 1 adult and 1 baby. Serve the adult portion with extra fruit and ice cream or yogurt.

Cover and keep in the refrigerator for up to 1 day.

Useful Notes
❄: Yes ✤: Yes

RASPBERRY DELIGHT

Makes about 36 tablespoons
PREPARATION TIME: 15 minutes plus setting time

This easy dessert is a great way of introducing fruit such as raspberries to your baby's diet. For an even speedier dessert, omit the apple juice and gelatin. Simply combine the strained raspberries, yogurt, and sugar, and serve immediately.

1¼ cups (310 ml) canned raspberries in juice

2 tsp. (10 ml) unflavored gelatin

100 ml (3½ fl oz) plus 2 tbsp. (30 ml) whole-milk plain yogurt

2 tbsp. (30 ml) sugar

⅔ cup (160 ml) unsweetened apple juice

1 Drain the raspberries, reserving the fruit and juice separately.

2 Place the raspberry juice in a small bowl and sprinkle the gelatin over the surface. Set aside for a couple of minutes until the gelatin is spongy.

3 Place the bowl over a pan of gently simmering water and stir the juice mixture until the gelatin has completely dissolved. Allow to cool slightly.

4 Press the raspberries through a strainer, reserving the fruit pulp and discarding all the seeds.

5 Blend the fruit pulp, yogurt, and sugar in a blender or food processor until smooth. Gradually blend in the gelatin mixture and apple juice until well mixed.

6 Pour the mixture into a serving dish and chill in the refrigerator for several hours or overnight, until lightly set.

Variations
Use other canned fruits, such as pitted plums or cherries, in place of the raspberries.
Use unsweetened orange or pineapple juice in place of the apple juice.

Cook's Tips
When using unflavored gelatin, always add gelatin to the liquid—never the other way round. Also, never allow the gelatin mixture to boil.
For vegetarians, gelatin-type products are available to use in place of gelatin.

Recipe can easily be adapted for an adult meal. This dessert will serve 2–3 adults and 1 baby. Serve the adult portions with wafer cookies, or fresh fruit, such as peach slices.
Cover and keep in the refrigerator for up to 1 day.

Nutrition Notes
Calcium: ▲   Vitamin C: ▲

Useful Notes
❋: No   ❋: No

MANGO WITH YOGURT

Makes about 25 tablespoons
PREPARATION TIME: 10 minutes

A quick-and-easy dessert which is full of flavor and one your baby is sure to enjoy. Choose a whole-milk fruit yogurt for this recipe, preferably one which is made especially for babies and toddlers.

1 medium-sized ripe mango

⅔ cup (180 ml) whole-milk apricot yogurt

4 tbsp. (60 ml) plain whole-milk yogurt

1 Peel and seed the mango and roughly chop the flesh. Place in a blender or food processor and blend until smooth.

2 Add the fruit yogurt and plain yogurt and blend until well mixed.

3 Pour into a serving dish and serve immediately, or cover and chill in the refrigerator for up to 1 day.

Variations

Use other fresh ripe fruit, such as banana, in place of the mango.

Use a flavored fruit yogurt of your choice, such as raspberry or strawberry, for a change.

Use canned mango in place of the fresh mango.

Cook's Tips

When selecting a mango, choose one which yields when gently squeezed in the palm of your hand.

Recipe can easily be adapted for an adult meal. This dessert will serve 1 adult and 1 baby. Serve the adult portion with extra fresh fruit.

Nutrition Notes

Calcium: ▲   Vitamin C: ▲

Useful Notes

❀: Yes   ❀: No

55

PEACH AND RASPBERRY FOOL

Makes about 20 tablespoons ✸ *PREPARATION TIME:* 10 minutes

A refreshingly light dessert with a nutritious combination of fresh fruit and yogurt, this fool is quick and easy to make and serve. For children, serve the fool with wafer cookies for an extra special treat. Try freezing this dessert and serve as a frozen ice, for a tasty change.

1¼ cups (310 ml) fresh ripe raspberries

¾ cup (180 ml) canned peach slices
in juice, drained

⅔ cup (160 ml) whole-milk plain yogurt

1 Mash the raspberries in a bowl, then press them through a strainer. Reserve the juice and pulp and discard the seeds.

2 Place the peaches in a blender or food processor and blend until smooth. Add the raspberry purée and blend until well mixed. Place the fruit mixture in a bowl.

3 Fold the yogurt into the fruit purée. Serve immediately or cover and chill.

Variations

Use other fresh fruit, such as strawberries or blackberries, in place of the raspberries.

Cook's Tips

The fruit juice drained from the peaches can be diluted with a little water and served as a refreshing drink.

Recipe can easily be adapted for an adult meal. This fool serves 1–2 adults and 1 baby. Serve the adult portion(s) with wafer cookies.

Cover and chill for up to 1 day.

☆
Nutrition Notes
Vitamin C: ▲

Useful Notes
: Yes ✸*: Yes*

APRICOT YOGURT FOOL

Makes about 16 tablespoons ❋ *PREPARATION TIME:* 10 minutes

Dried fruit purées, such as this dried apricot purée, make an ideal base for desserts for your baby. Combined with whole-milk yogurt, this creamy apricot fool could not be easier to make, and is simply delicious.

¹/₂ cup (125 ml) chopped ready-to-eat dried apricots

4 tbsp. (60 ml) freshly squeezed orange juice

²/₃ cup (160 ml) whole-milk plain yogurt

1 Place the apricots and orange juice in a blender or food processor and blend until smooth. Spoon into a bowl.

2 Fold the yogurt into the apricot purée and mix well. Serve immediately or cover and chill before serving.

Variations

Use other ready-to-eat dried fruits, such as pears, peaches, or prunes, in place of the apricots.

❋

Cook's Tips

Dried fruit, such as apricots or mixed dried fruit, are delicious when soaked in fruit juice overnight to make a delicious compote. The dried fruit and fruit juice can also be heated, then left to cool and soak overnight. Make up a larger batch of dried fruit compote, purée enough for your baby, and serve the rest with premium yogurt for a quick-and-easy dessert for your family to enjoy.

Recipe can easily be adapted for an adult meal. This fool will serve 1 adult and 1 baby. Serve the adult portion with wafer cookies.

Cover and keep in the refrigerator for up to 1 day.

Nutrition Notes

Calcium: ▲   Vitamin C: ▲

Useful Notes

: Yes   ❋: Yes

CHAPTER 3
9–12 MONTHS

MOVING ON TO FAMILY FOODS

Over the last three months of your baby's first year, you will be completing the final stage of the weaning process. So, by the time your baby is about 12 months of age, she should be eating more or less the same food as the rest of the family, but in a chopped-up form. During this important transitional phase, introduce a wider variety of foods, presented in an appealing way. Focus on encouraging your baby to feed herself by offering fun finger foods. The following introduction before the recipes offers practical advice on successfully achieving the move to family foods.

FAMILY MEALTIMES

Now you can start to prepare dishes you know the whole family will enjoy and will be ideal for your baby. The techniques are simple—remove your baby's portion before adding any seasoning, and roughly mash or chop up the food before serving it. In this way, your baby will enjoy interesting and varied meals, without the need for you to prepare separate dishes. Mealtimes should be sociable, so eat together as a family as often as you can.

Learning to feed themselves
Babies at this stage often refuse food given to them on a spoon and want to feed themselves. This is all part of their development, and it's important to encourage independent feeding. It usually results in messy mealtimes, with more food on the bib and floor than in their mouths! Sometimes it may seem as if your baby has eaten very little, so it might help to have two spoons, one for your baby to feed herself with and one for you to make sure some food goes into her mouth.

Finger foods also help to encourage self-feeding, and by now, your baby will be using her hands to feed herself, so try to include some finger foods at each

meal. We suggested a number of finger foods in chapter 2 (see page 41); you might also like to include soft cubes of well-cooked meat, cheese, or potato (cooked), as well as pieces of fruit and vegetables. Do not leave your baby alone when feeding, in case she chokes.

Think about the presentation of food now. Consider the combinations of colors, textures, and shapes of different foods and how they will look on the plate. Prepare our Salmon and Herb Fish Cakes with Tomato Salsa (page 66), or make the Strawberry Yogurt Gelatin (page 72) for visual appeal as well as taste. We have also included serving suggestions with the recipes in this chapter, which will give you

some more ideas for presentation. If you have a freezer, you could start freezing foods in larger containers, such as yogurt pots or small plastic or foil containers.

Foods to offer
By now, your baby should be accustomed to a wide variety of different foods, and enjoying three good meals a day, probably with light snacks and/or drinks in between. See below for ideas for suitable snacks and drinks. Try to offer a good mix of foods at each meal with more texture than previously, so that most foods can be mashed or chopped, such as lightly cooked vegetables and fresh fruit. Meat, however, should continue to be well cooked, and mashed or ground. Use the guide below to give you an idea of the number of servings to offer your baby from the different food groups. The actual amount of food eaten at each meal will vary—your baby's appetite should be your guide.

Starchy foods: These include bread, pasta, potato, rice, and cereals, including breakfast cereals. Try to offer whole-wheat varieties of bread, pasta, and rice on some occasions, and avoid the very sugary breakfast cereals. *Offer 3–4 servings of these starchy foods daily, and include some with each meal.*

Fruits and vegetables: Offer a wide variety of different fruits and vegetables, especially lightly cooked or raw, because they have a higher vitamin content than canned ones. Fruit and vegetables make ideal finger foods. Including fruit and vegetables that are high in vitamin C at mealtimes helps the absorption of iron. Diluted unsweetened orange juice can also be given. *Include 3–4 servings every day.*

Meat and meat alternatives: Offer a variety of meats, beans, legumes, eggs, and fish (including oily fish). If you are following a vegetarian diet, include mixtures of vegetable proteins, such as beans or legumes, with starchy foods, such as rice or bread, to make sure your baby gets all the protein she needs. *Include at least 1 serving of animal protein daily (meat, fish, or egg), or 2 servings of vegetable proteins.*

Milk and dairy foods: 2¼–2½ cups (560–625 ml) breast milk or infant formula should be drunk daily, so milk is still an important part of your baby's diet. Whole cows' milk or any of the above can also be used to mix with solids, or to make milk puddings and sauces. Whole-milk yogurt and hard cheeses can also be included, providing a useful source of protein and calcium, and can be used in place of some of the milk.

Other foods: Foods from the four food groups above should make up the bulk of your baby's diet, providing her with all the nutrients she needs to grow and stay healthy. Additional foods such as small amounts of oils and fats for cooking, for example pure vegetable oils and margarine or butter, can also be

included now, but still discourage sweet cookies, cakes, candies, chocolate, and salty foods. If candies and chocolates are given, try to save them for mealtimes only; don't offer them as special treats (see opposite for alternative ideas for between-meal snacks).

Drinks

The same advice applies here for recommended drinks as in the previous chapter (see page 41). Milk or water should be offered between meals (but try not to offer milk to drink just before a meal, because this may spoil your baby's appetite), and unsweetened, diluted fruit juice or water at mealtimes. Milk can also be offered as a drink at mealtimes, preferably after food. Whole cows' milk is not suitable as a main drink until your baby is about a year old. Sweetened drinks, carbonated drinks, and fruit juices offered between meals are not good for healthy teeth, and can have an adverse effect even before, or just as, teeth are showing through gums.

Ideas for between-meal snacks

If your baby is hungry between meals, try offering some of the following:
* slices of fresh fruit, such as peeled apple, peaches, pear, melon, banana, and avocado
* cubes of lightly cooked or raw vegetables, such as slices of red or yellow pepper, baby corn, carrot, and peeled cucumber
* rice cakes
* fingers of bread or toast, plain or spread with soft cheese or hummus, for example
* bagels
* whole-milk yogurt (low-fat varieties are not suitable)
* cubes of hard, mild cheese
* chopped hard-cooked egg
* cold, cooked pasta shapes
* plain cookies, crackers, fruit muffins, plain cake, biscuits, or tea cakes

Food fads

Sometimes babies who have been good eaters suddenly start refusing food around this time, or reject milk as a drink. This can be distressing for you as a parent, but it is usually only a temporary phase and may be a case of your baby exerting her independence. We discuss this more in the next chapter (see pages 80–82). If she has temporarily lost her appetite, offer her favorite foods, and something which does not require a lot of chewing. If you are concerned, consult your pediatrician or a dietitian.

If your baby rejects milk as a drink, offer other dairy products, especially cheese and whole-milk yogurts, to make sure she gets the calcium she needs. Look at our dessert recipes in this chapter and the previous chapter (pages 42–57) for lots of ideas for including yogurt in a variety of dishes. You can also disguise milk in both sweet and savory sauces. Use the recipes marked as good sources of calcium.

SPRING VEGETABLE OMELET

PORTIONS: Makes about 6 ✿ *PREPARATION TIME:* 15 minutes ✿ *COOKING TIME:* 6–8 minutes

This colorful omelet is ideal for both babies and young children. Make sure the egg is well cooked—both egg white and yolk should be hard cooked. Finely chop or roughly mash before serving to your baby with toast fingers or fresh bread. This can be served hot or at room temperature.

1 Place the eggs and milk in a large measuring jug and beat together.

2 Add all the remaining ingredients, except the oil, and mix well.

3 Heat a little oil in a 7-inch (18-cm) nonstick omelet pan. Pour in the beaten egg mixture and cook over medium heat until golden brown underneath and the egg is well cooked.

4 Place the pan under a preheated medium broiler and broil for a few minutes, until golden brown and set on top.

5 Cut into wedges to serve and roughly chop before serving.

❦

Variations

Use 1 tsp. (5 ml) Italian seasoning in place of the fresh herbs.

Use 1 shallot, finely chopped, in place of the scallions.

Use other hard cheese, such as Colby or Swiss, in place of the cheddar.

✿

Cook's Tips

Recipe can easily be adapted for an adult meal. This omelet will serve 1–2 adults and 1 baby.

☆

Nutrition Notes

Calcium: ▲   *Vitamin C:* ▲▲

✐

Useful Notes

✿: *Yes*   ✿: *No*

2 eggs	*1/3 cup (80 ml) finely chopped, seeded red pepper*
1 tbsp. (15 ml)) milk	*3 tbsp. (45 ml) frozen peas or petit pois*
2 scallions, finely chopped	*3 tbsp. (45 ml) grated cheddar cheese*
1 tomato, skinned, seeded, and finely chopped	*1 tbsp. (15 ml) chopped fresh mixed herbs or parsley*
1 small carrot, coarsely grated	*a little sunflower oil, for frying*
1 baby zucchini, coarsely chopped	

TURKEY STIR-FRY

PORTIONS: Makes about 7 ✿ *PREPARATION TIME:* 15 minutes ✿ *COOKING TIME:* 10 minutes

A quick-and-easy dish to prepare and make, this appetizing stir-fry is sure to be a favorite with the whole family. Choose your own selection of vegetables in season for variety.

1 tsp. (5 ml) cornstarch

2 tbsp. (30 ml) unsweetened apple juice

2 tbsp. (30 ml) vegetable or chicken stock (see page 14)

1 tbsp. (15 ml) tomato ketchup

2 tsp. (10 ml) olive oil

4 oz. (115 g) skinless, boneless turkey breast half, cut into thin strips

4 scallions, finely chopped

½ cup (125 ml) finely chopped yellow pepper

⅓ cup (80 ml) finely chopped snow peas

1 small carrot, finely chopped

⅓ cup (80 ml) shredded cabbage

¼ cup (40 ml) chopped beansprouts

1 In a small bowl, blend the cornstarch with the apple juice, stock, and tomato ketchup and set aside.

2 Heat the oil in a nonstick skillet or wok. Add the turkey and stir-fry over medium heat for 2 minutes.

3 Add all the vegetables to the pan and stir-fry for 5–7 minutes longer, or until the turkey and vegetables are cooked through and very tender.

4 Add the cornstarch mixture and continue to stir-fry the ingredients until the sauce is thickened and glossy.

5 Chop the turkey before serving and serve with boiled rice.

Variations

Use chicken or lean pork in place of the turkey.

Use unsweetened orange or grape juice in place of the apple juice.

Cook's Tips

Recipe can easily be adapted for an adult meal. This stir-fry will serve 1 adult and 1 baby. Serve the adult portion with boiled rice or pasta and a mixed leaf salad.

☆

Nutrition Notes

Vitamin C: ▲▲

Useful Notes

❋: *No*   ✿: *No*

MINI MEATBALLS IN HERBY TOMATO SAUCE

PORTIONS: Makes about 9 ❂ *PREPARATION TIME:* 25 minutes, plus 20 minutes chilling time ❂ *COOKING TIME:* 45 minutes

Babies and young children will love these mini meatballs, served in a herb-flavored tomato sauce. Served with cooked fresh seasonal vegetables, you can enjoy them, too.

For the meatballs:

¹/₂ lb. (250 g) lean minced pork

2 shallots, finely chopped

³/₄ cup (180 ml) finely chopped mushrooms

1 tsp. (5 ml) dried oregano

1 tsp. (5 ml) dried thyme

¹/₂ cup (125 ml) fresh whole-wheat bread crumbs

1 tbsp. (15 ml) tomato ketchup

¹/₂ tsp. (2.5 ml)) tomato paste

a little flour, for dusting

1 tbsp. (15 ml) sunflower oil

For the tomato sauce:

1 cup (250 ml) canned chopped tomatoes

²/₃ cup (160 ml) vegetable stock (see page 14)

2 shallots, finely chopped

1 tbsp. (15 ml) tomato ketchup

dash of Worcestershire sauce

1–2 tbsp. (15-30 ml) chopped fresh mixed herbs

1 To make the meatballs, place all the ingredients, except the flour and oil, in a bowl and mix thoroughly.

2 With floured hands, roll the meatball mixture into about 18 small balls and roll each ball lightly in flour. Place on a plate, cover, and chill in the refrigerator for 20 minutes.

3 Heat the oil in a skillet and gently fry the meatballs over medium heat for 5–10 minutes, turning them frequently, until they are lightly browned all over.

Variations

Use lean ground beef or chicken in place of the pork.

Use 1 small onion in place of the shallots.

Use fresh parsley in place of the mixed herbs.

❂

Cook's Tips

The tomato sauce may be puréed in a blender or food processor before heating, if you like.

Recipe can easily be adapted for an adult meal. This recipe will serve 2 adults and 1 baby. Serve the adult portions with boiled brown rice and stir-fried vegetables.

Useful Notes

❀: No   ❂: Yes

Carefully transfer the meatballs to a shallow, ovenproof dish Set the dish aside and keep warm.

4 To make the tomato sauce, strain the tomatoes, discarding the seeds. Place the tomato juice and pulp in a saucepan with the remaining ingredients and stir thoroughly to mix. Cover the pan and bring to a boil over medium heat, stirring occasionally.

5 Pour the tomato sauce over the meatballs, cover, and bake in a preheated oven at 350°F (180°C) for about 45 minutes.

6 Roughly chop the meatballs before serving and serve with mashed potatoes and boiled or steamed broccoli flowerets.

SPAGHETTI AND SAUCE

PORTIONS: Makes about 10 portions of sauce ✹ *PREPARATION TIME:* 15 minutes ✹ *COOKING TIME:* 1½ hours

An old favorite with children and adults, this traditional pasta sauce can be served with white or whole-wheat spaghetti or another pasta of your choice.

½ lb. (250 g) lean ground beef

1 onion, finely chopped

1 clove garlic, crushed

2 small carrots, finely chopped

2 celery stalks, finely chopped

2½ cups (725 ml) finely chopped mushrooms

1 cup (250 ml) canned chopped tomatoes, strained and seeds discarded

½ cup (125 ml) beef stock (see page 14)

½ cup (125 ml) unsweetened apple or grape juice

1 tbsp. (15 ml) tomato ketchup

1 bay leaf

½–1oz. (15–30 g) whole-wheat spaghetti, for 1 baby serving

1 Place the ground beef, chopped onion, and garlic in a saucepan and cook gently, stirring frequently, until the beef is browned all over.

2 Add all the remaining ingredients, except the spaghetti, and stir to mix.

3 Cover, bring to a boil, then simmer for 1½ hours, or until the meat and vegetables are cooked and tender, stirring occasionally. Discard the bay leaf.

4 Meanwhile, cook the spaghetti in a saucepan of boiling water for 10–12 minutes, until cooked and tender.

5 Drain the spaghetti and serve with the meat sauce spooned over. Chop the spaghetti before serving it to your baby.

Variations

Use ground chicken or turkey in place of the beef.

Use 1 tsp. (5 ml) Italian seasoning in place of the bay leaf.

Use white spaghetti or tagliatelle in place of the whole-wheat spaghetti.

Cook's Tips

The cooked sauce can be cooled slightly, then puréed and reheated thoroughly before serving, if you like.

Recipe can easily be adapted for an adult meal. The meat sauce will serve 1–2 adults and 1 baby. Serve the adult portions with boiled spaghetti and garlic bread. Allow 3–4 oz. (85–115 g) dried pasta per adult serving.

Nutrition Notes

Vitamin C: ▲

Useful Notes

❀: No   ✿: Yes, but the sauce only

SALMON AND HERB FISH CAKES WITH TOMATO SALSA

PORTIONS: Makes 8 fish cakes ✸ *PREPARATION TIME:* 15 minutes plus 30 minutes chilling time ✸ *COOKING TIME:* 10 minutes

The simple fish shape of these delicious fish cakes is sure to attract your baby's attention. Try using pieces of fresh vegetables to make a face on each fish, for extra appeal.

For the fish cakes:	squeeze of fresh lemon juice	For the tomato salsa:
1 leek, washed and finely chopped	1 egg, beaten	3 plum tomatoes, skinned and seeded
1 cup (250 ml) cold cooked, mashed potatoes	fresh whole-wheat breadcrumbs, for coating	1 tbsp. (15 ml) tomato ketchup
½ cup (125 ml) canned pink salmon in water	sunflower oil, for frying	
1 tbsp. (15 ml) chopped fresh parsley		1 tbsp. (15 ml) chopped fresh parsley

66

1 To make the fish cakes, cook the chopped leek in boiling water for about 10 minutes, until tender. Drain well and squeeze out any excess water.

2 Mix the mashed potatoes with the leeks.

3 Drain and flake the salmon, discarding any bones. Mix into the potato mixture with the parsley and lemon juice.

4 On a lightly floured surface, shape the mixture into 8 fish shapes or rounds.

5 Dip each fish cake in the egg and then the bread crumbs. Place on a plate, cover, and refrigerate for 30 minutes.

6 Heat a little oil in a nonstick skillet, add the fish cakes, and cook, turning once, until crisp and golden on both sides.

7 Meanwhile, make the tomato salsa. Chop the tomato flesh finely and place in a bowl. Add the tomato ketchup and parsley and stir to mix.

8 Roughly chop and serve the cooked fish cakes with some of the tomato salsa spooned alongside. Serve with boiled peas or other cooked seasonal vegetables, such as diced, boiled carrots.

Variations

Use other fish canned in water, such as red salmon or tuna, in place of the pink salmon.

Use standard tomatoes in place of the plum tomatoes for the salsa.

Cook's Tips

It is essential that all fish bones are removed.

The fish cakes can be brushed lightly with oil and broiled rather than fried, if you prefer.

Recipe can easily be adapted for an adult meal. This recipe will serve 2 adults and 1 baby.

Nutrition Notes

Salmon is a good source of the fat-soluble vitamins A, D, and E.

Useful Notes

❀: *No* ❀: *Yes*

BAKED COD WITH CHEESE AND CORN SAUCE

PORTIONS: Makes about 9 ❂ PREPARATION TIME: 10 minutes ❂ COOKING TIME: 20–30 minutes

A simple, yet delicious, way of serving fish. We have used cod fillets in this recipe but other white fish such as haddock or flounder works just as well. Serve with potatoes or fingers of toast, and lightly cooked vegetables.

squeeze of fresh lemon juice

6 oz. (180 g) skinless cod fillets

1 tbsp. (15 ml) butter or margarine

1 tbsp. (15 ml) all-purpose flour

1 cup (250 ml) milk

1 cup (250 ml) canned, drained corn kernels

1/3 cup (80 ml) grated cheddar cheese

1–2 tbsp. (15–30 ml) chopped fresh parsley

1 Squeeze a little fresh lemon juice over each cod fillet, then loosely wrap each fillet in a piece of greased foil.

2 Place the foil parcels on a baking sheet and bake in a preheated oven at 350°F (180°C) for 20–30 minutes, or until cooked through.

3 Meanwhile, make the cheese and corn sauce. Place the butter or margarine, flour, and milk together in a saucepan. Heat gently, whisking continuously, until the sauce comes to a boil and thickens. Simmer the sauce gently for 2 minutes, stirring continuously.

4 Add the drained corn kernels and heat gently until thoroughly hot, stirring continuously.

5 Remove the saucepan from the heat and stir in the grated cheese and the finely chopped fresh parsley. Mix well.

6 Roughly chop the fish fillets and serve them with the cheese and corn sauce poured over.

Variations

Use other cheese such as Monterey jack in place of the cheddar cheese.

Cook's Tips

Recipe can easily be adapted for an adult meal. This recipe will serve 2 adults and 1 baby.

Nutrition Notes

Calcium: ▲

Useful Notes

❀: *No* ❀: *Yes*

SWEET POTATO AND CHICK-PEA BAKE

PORTIONS: Makes about 9 ✿ *PREPARATION TIME:* 20 minutes ✿ *COOKING TIME:* 45–60 minutes

Sweet potato may already be a favorite food; it combines beautifully with lots of different savory foods. Here, we've teamed it up with chick-peas and vegetables for a flavorful, nutritious dish.

12 oz. (350 g) sweet potato, peeled and thinly sliced

1 tbsp. (15 ml) olive oil

2 tsp. (10 ml) sunflower oil

1 leek, washed and chopped

1½ cups (375 ml) sliced mushrooms

1 tbsp. (15 ml) butter or margarine

1 tbsp. (15 ml) all-purpose flour

⅔ cup (160 ml) milk

½ cup (125 ml) vegetable stock (see page 14), cooled

½ cup (125 ml) grated cheddar cheese

½ cup (125 ml) canned, drained chick-peas

½ cup (125 ml) canned, drained corn kernels

½ cup (125 ml) frozen petit pois

1 Parboil the potato slices in a saucepan of boiling water for 3 minutes. Drain well, then toss the slices thoroughly in the olive oil and set aside.

2 Heat the sunflower oil in a saucepan, add the leek and mushrooms, cover, and cook gently for about 10 minutes, or until all the vegetables are cooked and tender, stirring occasionally.

3 Meanwhile, place the butter or margarine, flour, milk, and stock in a saucepan. Heat gently, whisking continuously, until the sauce comes to a boil and thickens. Simmer gently for 2 minutes, stirring continuously.

4 Remove the pan from the heat, add the cheese, and stir until melted. Stir the chick-peas and all the vegetables, except the potato slices, into the cheese sauce and stir until well mixed.

5 Spoon the vegetable mixture into an ovenproof dish and arrange the potato slices in a layer over the top, covering the mixture completely.

6 Cover with foil and bake in a preheated oven at 400°F (200°C) for 45–60 minutes. Remove the foil for the last 20 minutes of the cooking time, to brown and crisp the top of the bake.

7 Roughly chop the bake before serving to your baby, and serve with a finely chopped mixed salad.

❧
Variations
Use your own choice of canned and frozen peas and beans.

Use zucchini in place of the mushrooms.

✿
Cook's Tips
Recipe can easily be adapted for an adult meal. This recipe will serve 2 adults and 1 baby. Serve the adult portions with a mixed side salad and warmed ciabatta bread.

Nutrition Notes
Calcium: ▲ Vitamin C: ▲

Useful Notes
: Yes ✿: Yes

PASTA TWISTS WITH ZUCCHINI AND PEPPERS

PORTIONS: Makes about 12 ❂ *PREPARATION TIME:* 10 minutes ❂ *COOKING TIME:* 10–12 minutes

Pasta is a highly nutritious (especially whole-wheat varieties), versatile food. With so many different shapes to choose from, it has great visual appeal and a wonderful texture which babies love, especially when feeding themselves. Pasta combined with a variety of sauces makes the choice of flavors endless.

1 cup (250 ml) whole-wheat pasta twists

2 tsp. (10 ml) olive oil

1 small onion, finely chopped

1 small clove garlic, crushed

1 zucchini, chopped

1 small red pepper, seeded and finely chopped

1½ cups (375 ml) sliced or chopped button mushrooms

1 cup (250 ml) canned chopped tomatoes, strained and seeds discarded

1 tbsp. (15 ml) tomato paste

1 tbsp. (15 ml) tomato ketchup

pinch of Italian seasoning

1 Cook the pasta twists in a large saucepan of boiling water for 10–12 minutes, or until cooked and tender.

2 Meanwhile, heat the oil in a nonstick skillet or wok. Add the onion, garlic, zucchini, pepper, and mushrooms and stir-fry for 3 minutes.

3 Reduce the heat slightly, add the tomato pulp and juice, tomato paste, tomato ketchup, and the Italian seasoning and cook for 4 minutes, stirring frequently, until the vegetables are cooked and tender.

4 Drain the pasta twists thoroughly. Add the drained pasta to the vegetable mixture, toss together to mix, and serve immediately. Roughly chop the pasta and vegetables before serving the dish to your baby.

Variations

Use white or tricolor pasta twists in place of the whole-wheat pasta.

Sprinkle with a little grated fresh Parmesan cheese before serving.

Cook's Tips

The cooked sauce can be cooled slightly, puréed, and reheated before mixing with the pasta.

Recipe can easily be adapted for an adult meal.

This recipe will serve 2 adults and 1 baby. Serve the adult portions with fresh crusty bread and a green side salad.

Nutrition Notes

Vitamin C: ▲

Useful Notes

: *Yes* : *Yes, but the sauce only*

MIXED BEAN AND VEGETABLE RISOTTO

PORTIONS: Makes about 12 ✸ *PREPARATION TIME:* 10 minutes ✸ *COOKING TIME:* 35 minutes

*A colorful mixture of textures and tastes, this risotto is a great way of encouraging your baby
to eat a whole variety of vegetables in one delicious meal! This recipe makes plenty of baby servings, making it
an ideal dish to prepare and cook for all the family to enjoy.*

1 Place the rice, onion, celery, carrot, mushrooms, kidney beans, stock, tomato paste, and herbs in a saucepan and mix.

2 Cover and bring to a boil, then simmer gently for 30–35 minutes, or until the rice and vegetables are cooked and tender, stirring occasionally.

3 Meanwhile, cook the green beans in a saucepan of boiling water for about 5 minutes, or until cooked and tender. Drain the beans thoroughly.

4 Stir the beans into the risotto and mix.

5 Roughly chop or mash before serving.

Variations

Use your own choice of vegetables and beans.

Use white rice in place of the brown rice.

✸

Cook's Tips

*Recipe can easily be adapted for an adult meal.
This risotto will serve 2 adults and 1 baby.
Serve the adult portions with thick slices of
fresh crusty bread.*

*Sprinkle with a little grated cheddar or
Parmesan cheese before serving.*

☆

Nutrition Notes
Vitamin C: ▲

Useful Notes
 ❀: *Yes* ✸: *Yes*

¹/₂ cup (125 ml) long-grain brown rice	¹/₃ cup (80 ml) canned, drained red kidney beans
1 small onion, finely chopped	1¹/₂ cups (375 ml) vegetable stock (see page 14)
2 celery stalks, finely chopped	¹/₂ tsp. (2.5 ml) tomato paste
1 carrot, finely chopped	1 tsp. (5 ml) dried Herbes de Provence
1¹/₂ cups (375 ml) sliced mushrooms	³/₄ cup (180 ml) chopped green beans

FRESH MUSHROOM SOUP

PORTIONS: Makes about 10 ✿ *PREPARATION TIME:* 10 minutes ✿ *COOKING TIME:* 20 minutes

Homemade soups are quick and easy to make, and are full of flavor and nutrients.
This delicious mushroom soup is an ideal way to introduce soup to your baby.
Serve with toast or bread cut into animal shapes, for extra appeal.

and celery and cook gently for 5 minutes, stirring occasionally.

2 Add the flour and cook gently for 1 minute, stirring. Gradually stir in the vegetable stock and milk and mix well.

3 Bring to a boil, stirring, then cover and simmer gently for about 15 minutes, or until the vegetables are cooked and tender, stirring occasionally.

4 Remove the pan from the heat and allow the soup to cool slightly, then purée it in a blender or food processor until smooth. Return the soup to the rinsed-out saucepan.

5 Add the chopped parsley and heat gently until the soup is piping hot, stirring. Ladle into a bowl to serve.

Variations

Use zucchini in place of the mushrooms.
Use fresh tarragon in place of the parsley.

Cook's Tips

The soup does not need to be blended before serving. Once cooked, simply serve as it is.
Recipe can easily be adapted for an adult meal. This soup will serve 2–3 adults and 1 baby.

Nutrition Notes

Calcium: ▲

Useful Notes

 ✿: Yes ✿: Yes

---

2 tbsp. (30 ml) butter or margarine

3¹/₄ cups (875 ml) finely chopped mushrooms

2 shallots, finely chopped

2 celery stalks, finely chopped

2 tbsp. (30 ml) all-purpose flour

1¹/₄ cups (310 ml) vegetable stock (see page 14)

1¹/₄ cups (310 ml) milk

2 tbsp. (30 ml) chopped fresh parsley

1 Melt the butter or margarine in a saucepan, add the mushrooms, shallots,

STRAWBERRY-YOGURT GELATIN

PORTIONS: Makes 6–8 small molded desserts   ✹   *PREPARATION TIME:* 10 minutes plus cooling and chilling time   ✹   *COOKING TIME:* 5 minutes

Molded desserts are always a popular choice with babies and young children, particularly when they taste as good as this one! Use a variety of different molds and decorate the yogurt forms just before serving.

1 standard package sweetened gelatin dessert mix

6 oz. (180 g) strawberries, hulled

1¼ cups (310 ml) whole-milk plain yogurt

1 Pour 1 cup (250 ml) hot water and 1 cup (250 ml) cold water into a small bowl. Add the powdered gelatin to the water and stir.

2 Continue to stir until the gelatin is thoroughly mixed with the water. Set aside to cool the mixture completely.

3 Place the strawberries in a blender or food processor and blend until smooth. Strain the strawberry mixture to remove some of the seeds.

4 Transfer the purée to the blender or food processor, add the cooled gelatin and yogurt, and blend until well mixed.

5 Pour into 6–8 small, wetted molds or 1 large mold and refrigerate until set.

6 Once set, unmold carefully onto serving plates and serve immediately. Decorate the desserts with colored icing and/or small candies before serving.

Variations

Use other fresh berries, such as blackberries or raspberries, in place of the strawberries.

Use a fruit-flavored whole-milk yogurt in place of the plain yogurt.

Cook's Tips

Recipe can easily be adapted for an adult meal. This recipe will serve 2–3 adults and 1 baby.

Cover and refrigerate for up to 1 day.

Useful Notes

Calcium: ▲   Vitamin C: ▲▲

Useful Notes

❄: No   ❄: No

CHOCOLATE-BANANA WHIP

PORTIONS: Makes about 8 ❂ *PREPARATION TIME:* 15 minutes

This quick-and-easy dessert brings together two favorite foods, making it a popular choice with babies, young children, and adults, too.

4 tbsp. (60 ml) semisweet chocolate chips

2 tbsp. (30 ml) light corn syrup

²/₃ cup (160 ml) crème fraîche (see below)

²/₃ cup (160 ml) whole-milk plain yogurt

2 bananas

1 Place the chocolate chips and syrup in a heatproof bowl and place the bowl over a pan of simmering water. Stir the ingredients until completely melted. Remove the pan from the heat.

2 Add the crème fraîche and stir the chocolate mixture until well blended. Remove the bowl from the saucepan.

3 Cool slightly, then stir in the yogurt. Peel and mash the bananas, then stir them into the chocolate mixture, stirring until thoroughly mixed.

4 Serve immediately or cover and chill before serving. Serve with extra slices of banana if you like.

Variations

Crème fraîche is a thick, slightly sour cream from France. If you cannot find it in delicatessens or gourmet food stores, combine 1 cup (250 ml) warmed whipping cream and 2 tbsp. (30 ml) buttermilk in a glass bowl. Let stand at room temperature for 24–48 hours until thick. Do not stir. Or substitute sour cream.

Cook's Tips

Slice or chop the bananas instead of mashing them and fold the sliced bananas into the chocolate mixture just before serving.

Recipe can easily be adapted for an adult meal. This recipe will serve 2 adults and 1 baby.

Serve the adult portions with extra fresh fruit, such as sliced apples, apricots, or pears.

Cover and keep in the refrigerator for up to 1 day.

Useful Notes
❂: Yes ❂: No

CHERRY BATTER DESSERT

PORTIONS: Makes about 8 ✿ *PREPARATION TIME:* 10 minutes ✿ *COOKING TIME:* 20–25 minutes

An appealing way of serving fruit to your baby, this batter dessert makes an appetizing addition to your baby's diet. It is equally delicious served warm or cold with ice cream.

scant 1/2 cups (125 ml) all-purpose flour

1 large egg, beaten

3/4 cup (180 ml) milk

2 tbsp. (30 ml) sugar

1 tbsp. (15 ml) sunflower oil

1 2/3 cups (400 ml) canned pitted cherries in juice

1 Sift the flour into a bowl and make a well in the center. Add the egg, then gradually beat in the milk, drawing the flour in from the sides to make a smooth batter. Add the sugar and mix well.

2 Place the oil in a nonstick, shallow 6 inch (15 cm) square cake pan and heat in a preheated oven at 425°F (220°C) for 2–3 minutes, or until hot.

3 Remove from the oven, scatter cherries over the base, then pour the batter over.

4 Bake for 20–25 minutes, or until risen and golden brown. Chop before serving.

Variations

Use whole-wheat flour in place of the white flour.

Use other fruits, such as fresh apple slices, apricot halves, or pitted plums, in place of the cherries.

Cook's Tips

Recipe can easily be adapted for an adult meal. This dessert will serve 2 adults and 1 baby.

Cool, cover, and keep in the refrigerator for up to 1 day.

Nutrition Notes
Iron: ▲

Useful Notes
❄: Yes   ✳: Yes

MIXED FRUIT COMPOTE

PORTIONS: Makes about 8 ✳ *PREPARATION TIME:* 15 minutes, plus standing time

*Fresh fruit is often best served simply chopped and tossed in a little fruit juice.
This fresh fruit compote is exactly that—simple and delicious.*

1/3 cup (80 ml) chopped strawberries

1/3 cup (80 ml) small raspberries

1 kiwi fruit, peeled and chopped

1 peach or nectarine, peeled, pitted, and chopped

1 small apple or pear, peeled, cored, and chopped

4 tbsp. (60 ml) unsweetened pineapple juice

4 tbsp. (60 ml) unsweetened orange juice

pinch of ground cinnamon or ginger (optional)

1 Place all the prepared fruit in a large bowl and gently stir to mix.

2 Mix together the fruit juices and cinnamon or ginger, if using. Pour over the fruit and gently stir to mix.

3 Cover and leave to stand for about 2 hours before serving. Serve with a small scoop of ice cream.

Variations

Use your own choice of fresh or canned fruits.

Use other combinations of unsweetened fruit juices, such as apple and grape juices.

Cook's Tips

This dessert can be served as soon as it is made, but it is best left to stand for a while to allow flavors to develop and mingle.

Recipe can easily be adapted for an adult meal. This compote will serve 1–2 adults and 1 baby.

Cover and keep in the refrigerator for up to 1 day.

Nutrition Notes
Vitamin C: ▲▲

Useful Notes
❄: Yes   ✳: No

PEAR AND APRICOT PUDDING

PORTIONS: Makes about 8 ✪ *PREPARATION TIME:* 15 minutes ✪ *COOKING TIME:* 1 hour

This fruity pudding is sure to be a favorite choice for your baby. Serve with ice cream.

1 small pear, peeled, cored, and sliced or chopped

4 canned apricot halves, chopped, plus 2 tbsp. (30 ml) apricot juice

4 tbsp. (60 ml) butter or margarine.

4 tbsp. (60 ml) sugar

1 egg, beaten

²/₃ cup (160 ml) self-rising flour, sifted

a little milk, to mix

76

1 Mix the pear slices or pieces and canned apricot halves together and place in the base of a lightly greased 2½-cup (675-ml) ovenproof bowl. Spoon the apricot juice over and set aside.

2 Cream the butter or margarine and sugar together until pale and fluffy. Gradually add the beaten egg, beating thoroughly after each addition.

3 Fold in the flour with enough milk to make a soft, dropping consistency.

4 Spoon the mixture into the prepared bowl over the fruit and smooth the surface. Cover with a double layer of pleated, greased, waxed or nonstick baking paper and secure with string.

5 Place the bowl in the top half of a steamer over a saucepan of boiling water. Cover with the lid and steam for about 1 hour, or until the pudding is well risen and cooked, topping up the pan with boiling water if necessary.

6 Carefully turn the pudding out onto a warmed serving plate and serve.

❤ Variations

Use 1 eating apple in place of the pear.

Add the finely grated peel of 1 lemon or ½ orange to the uncooked pudding batter, for extra delicious flavor.

Use half all-purpose and half whole-wheat flour.

✿ Cook's Tips

Recipe can easily be adapted for an adult meal. This pudding will serve 2 adults and 1 baby.

Cool, cover, and keep in the refrigerator for up to 1 day.

✎ Useful Notes

❄: Yes ✽: Yes

STRAWBERRY RICE PUDDING

PORTIONS: Makes about 4 ❂ *PREPARATION TIME:* 10 minutes
COOKING TIME: 1½–2 hours

This rice-based dessert is easy to prepare and is equally good served warm or cold.

2 tbsp. (30 ml) short-grain rice

1¼ cups (310 ml) milk

knob of butter or margarine

3 tbsp. (45 ml) whole-milk plain yogurt

⅓ cup (80 ml) ripe chopped strawberries

1 Place the rice and milk in a lightly greased, ovenproof dish and stir well to mix. Dot the surface of the rice mixture with the butter or margarine.

2 Bake in a preheated oven at 300°F (150°C) for about 30 minutes, then stir the mixture thoroughly. Bake for 1–1½ hours longer, or until the rice is cooked and tender and the mixture is thick and creamy.

3 Remove from the oven and set aside to cool a little. Once cool, stir in the yogurt and strawberries, mixing well. Serve immediately or chill before serving.

❤ Variations

Use other fresh fruits, such as raspberries, apricots, or peaches, in place of the strawberries.

Omit the yogurt and serve the rice pudding hot. Fold the strawberries into the rice pudding with a little strawberry jam, if you like, just before serving.

Cook's Tips

Recipe can easily be adapted for an adult meal. This dessert will serve 1 adult and 1 baby. Serve with extra fresh fruit, such as strawberries or raspberries.

Cool, cover, and keep for up to 1 day in the refrigerator.

☆ Nutrition Notes

Calcium: ▲ Vitamin C: ▲

✎ Useful Notes

❄: Yes ✽: No

CHAPTER 4
1–5 YEARS

HEALTHY EATING FOR TODDLERS

The 1–5 age range is a period of rapid development for young children, both physically and emotionally, and nutritional needs continue to be high—your child's weight is likely to increase by 80% and her height by 40% during this time. To meet these nutritional demands, it's important to offer your toddler a range of exciting, delicious, and, at the same time, healthy meals and snacks. At this age, food and eating can also provide exciting opportunities for learning, because toddlers can help with cooking and shopping, making food a fun and enjoyable experience in every way.

FAVORITE FOODS AND FADS

While you will be doing your best to continue to nurture good eating habits, prepare yourself for an obstacle. Toddlers very often feel the need to assert their independence, and may refuse to eat. But help is at hand..!

You may have already noticed how early your child has developed her own food likes and dislikes. If you have provided a variety of flavorful, nourishing dishes from early on, hopefully she will now be enjoying most foods. You can serve favorite foods often, but also try experimenting with new tastes and different ways of cooking and preparing foods. We've come up with a selection of delicious recipes designed to tempt young children and adults alike, using a variety of healthy ingredients. Encourage your child to join in when preparing some of the dishes in this chapter (such as Banana Tea Loaf and Apple and Apricot Crumble, pages 100–101), and enjoy sharing this time together.

Foods to offer

There is no need to prepare special foods for your toddler, once weaning is complete (around 18 months of age). Although the recipes in this chapter are designed to appeal to toddlers' taste buds, they can also be enjoyed by the whole family. Some toddlers survive happily on three meals a day, but many have small appetites relative to their size, and prefer to eat small meals with snacks in between. Either way, you can start good eating habits early on, by offering healthy snacks between meals, and a variety of foods at mealtimes, to guarantee a balanced diet. Use the guide below to help you to plan your toddlers' daily diet.

Starchy foods: Include at least one serving at each meal occasion, especially whole-wheat varieties of bread, pasta, rice, and cereals. *Offer 6 or more servings daily.*

Vegetables and fruit: Offer a variety of fresh, raw, or lightly cooked vegetables and fruit of normal adult texture. Frozen fruit and vegetables, canned fruit in fruit juice, and unsweetened fruit juice are also suitable. *Include 4 or more servings daily.*

Meat and meat alternatives: Try introducing more variety, such as oily fish (mackerel, salmon, sardines, and herring), and offer lean meat (cut off any visible fat on meat and buy lean cuts), or beans and legumes in stews and casseroles. *Include at least 1 serving of meat, fish, or egg, or 2 servings of vegetable proteins (dried peas, dried beans, and lentils).*

Milk and dairy foods: Whole cows' milk can be given as a drink at this age, and 2% milk can be used in cooking (rather than as a main drink). However, do not serve more than 2½ cups (625 ml) of milk to drink a day, because serving more than this amount can spoil your child's appetite for foods. *Include a minimum of 1½ cups (375 ml) of milk every day, or 2 servings of dairy products, such as yogurt or cheese.*

Other foods: Try to limit salty, savory snacks, such as potato chips, and sugary foods. Offer sugary foods at mealtimes if you want to include them, rather than as between-meal snacks. See "Tempting Toddler Snacks" below for healthy alternatives to high-sugar, high-salt foods.

Low-fat diets for toddlers?

Fat provides an important source of energy (calories) for growing, active children, yet after the age of 2, low-fat diets are generally recommended. Skim milk is now an acceptable drink for your child, providing she is obtaining adequate calories to fuel her growing body from other food sources.

A reminder about iron

In chapter 2 we talked in detail about the important role of iron in mental development during early childhood, when babies over 6 months can be vulnerable to a low-iron status. Toddlers, too, can be at risk of iron deficiency, so make sure you include some iron-containing foods on a regular basis in your child's diet. Look for those recipes in this chapter that indicate a useful or rich source of iron, and follow the nutritional guidelines above.

In order to prevent iron deficiency in young children, make sure that you include some, or preferably most, of the foods listed above on a regular basis in your toddler's diet. The recipes included in this chapter use a variety of the foods specified above.

- some meat (red meat and/or liver); poultry; fish, especially oily fish such as tuna, sardines, or salmon; or hard-cooked egg most days
- beans and legumes, such as lentils, chick-peas, red kidney beans, or baked beans, especially if meat is not eaten
- dried fruit, such as apricots, prunes, raisins, golden raisins, or foods containing them
- dark green vegetables, such as broccoli, spring greens, spinach, and peas
- some iron-fortified foods, especially breakfast cereals
- whole-grain rice, pasta, whole-wheat, and mixed-grain breads
- a source of vitamin C with meals containing beans, legumes, vegetables, or cereals to enhance the absorption of iron from these foods

Tempting toddler snacks

For those toddlers who are full of energy and may genuinely feel hungry between meals, try to encourage the eating of healthy snacks, and avoid (whenever possible!) letting them eat sweets, potato chips, and cookies. Listed here are a few suggestions:

- peeled fresh fruit, such as a small banana, apple wedges, orange or satsuma segments, and sliced seedless grapes
- raw peeled vegetables, such as red or yellow pepper slices, cucumber or carrots cut into small sticks, and celery sticks filled with soft cheese or smooth peanut butter
- breadsticks, rice cakes, fingers of lightly toasted bread, crackers spread with a cheese spread, and mini pita breads
- plain yogurt with pieces of fresh

fruit or cubes of cheese
• milk shake (see page 121 for ideas)
• Mini Biscuits (see page 120 for recipe)
• Banana Tea Loaf or Carrot and Golden Raisin Fingers (see pages 100–101 for recipe)

Many of these foods can form the basis of a healthy snack meal or lunch. Try offering mini sandwiches as well (see pages 110-111 for filling ideas) and serve with vegetable sticks, as above, or a yogurt or milk shake, with some fresh fruit, for a healthy, well-balanced meal.

Drinks for toddlers
Fluids are an essential part of everyone's diet, and your toddler is no exception. Even if your child does not feel hungry between meals, she should be offered a drink. Remember, the more often your child drinks or eats sugary foods or drinks throughout the day, the more damage is likely to occur to her teeth. Keep any sugary foods or drinks to meal-times if possible.

Milk, water, unsweetened diluted fruit juice, or sugar-free drinks are suitable between-meal drinks, but try not to offer them just before a meal, since this can spoil your child's appetite.

Note: During sleep, the protective flow of saliva over the teeth slows down, leaving teeth more vulnerable to sugar in the mouth. Make sure your child brushes her teeth after her bedtime drink.

Looking after young teeth
• As soon as the first tooth appears, start to clean it using a soft brush.
• If your water supply is not fluoridated, ask your pediatrician or dentist about fluoride drops, because fluoride helps to protect teeth from decay.
• Limit the serving of sugary foods and drinks to mealtimes—the more frequent the intake of sugar or sugary

foods/drinks, the more likely tooth damage will occur.

Fussy eaters: A parent's survival guide
It's normal for every child to have periods when she refuses certain foods, or possibly all foods for a brief while, but this phase should soon pass. Although this can be an anxious time for parents,

missing the odd meal won't do any harm to your child in the short term. If your child still seems lively and happy between mealtimes, there's no need to worry. If, however, the problem persists, and your child's normal weight gain begins to be affected, talk to your physician or a dietitian who will be able to give you expert advice.

TIPS ON OVERCOMING FOOD FADS

There are practical ways of trying to cope with food fads, which might help to overcome a difficult feeding phase, so try a few of the tips we've listed here for happier mealtimes:

• Have regular mealtimes and sit down together as a family to eat if you can. Children are great mimics—if they see you eating, they may also want to eat.
• Don't eat in the vicinity of obvious distractions, such as television.
• Don't spend ages preparing food if you know it's likely to be rejected—keep it simple.
• Keep to foods you know your child normally enjoys and include some finger foods because these are easy to eat (see page 41 for ideas).
• Offer regular meals and snacks at set times, and don't be tempted to let your child fill up on cookies, cakes, and potato chips throughout the day (see page 81 and above for "Tempting Toddler Snacks").
• Be careful not to allow your child to drink too much milk during the day (no more than about 2¹/₂ cups/375 ml milk a day)—it might be filling her up too much between meals.
• Offer small, attractive portions of food arranged on a small plate (she can always ask for more if she's still hungry).
• Leave the food out for about 20

minutes, while you have your meal, and try not to show that you're worried or anxious by your child not eating.
• Encourage and praise her when she does eat some food, however little, but don't make a fuss if there is still some left at the end of a meal. You could ask in a relaxed way if she wants any more, before removing the plate.
• Never force your child to eat. Even if you do coax her to swallow some food this time, you'll have to face the same drama next time around.
• Don't be tempted to use food as a reward ("if you eat up your vegetables you can have some ice cream/candy"). Instead, offer to play a favorite game, or take her somewhere special.
• If food is refused completely at a meal, don't allow your child to fill up on potato chips, cakes, or cookies instead, because this might become a habit—refusing food knowing that she can have whatever snack she wants afterward. If you want to give something, have a selection of fruit, vegetables, or drinks on hand for between-meal snacks.

CHICKEN FINGERS WITH BARBECUE SAUCE

PORTIONS: Makes about 4 ✪ *PREPARATION TIME:* 25 minutes ✪ *COOKING TIME:* 10–15 minutes

An appetizing way to serve chicken with a full-flavored homemade barbecue sauce, which will have appeal to toddlers and adults alike.

For the chicken fingers:

¹/₂ lb. (250 g) skinless, boneless chicken breast halves, cut into strips

1 tbsp. (15 ml) all-purpose flour

¹/₂ cup (125 ml) dry whole-wheat bread crumbs

2 tbsp. (30 ml) chopped fresh parsley

1 small egg, beaten

a little sunflower oil, for frying

For the barbecue sauce:

1 cup (250 ml) canned chopped tomatoes

2 shallots, finely chopped

1 clove garlic, crushed

2 tbsp. (30 ml) unsweetened pineapple juice

1 tbsp. (15 ml) red-wine vinegar

1 tbsp. (15 ml) light soft brown sugar

1 tsp. (5 ml) Worcestershire sauce

1 tsp. (5 ml) English mustard

1 To make the chicken fingers, dip the chicken in the flour, covering them completely, then shake off any excess flour.

2 Mix together the bread crumbs and chopped parsley. Dip the floured chicken strips in the beaten egg, then quickly roll in the bread crumb mixture, coating the chicken pieces completely.

3 Place on a plate, cover, and chill in the refrigerator for 15 minutes.

4 Meanwhile, make the barbecue sauce. Place all the sauce ingredients in a saucepan and stir to mix. Cover, bring to a boil, then simmer for 10 minutes, stirring occasionally. Uncover and simmer for 15 minutes longer, stirring occasionally.

5 In the meanwhile, heat a little oil in a nonstick skillet and cook the chicken strips over medium heat for 10–15 minutes, until cooked and golden brown, turning frequently.

6 Serve the chicken fingers with the barbecue sauce alongside. Serve with boiled or steamed carrots, or another vegetable of your choice, and boiled new potatoes tossed in chopped fresh parsley.

Variations

Use turkey breast or white fish, such as cod or haddock, in place of the chicken.

Use fresh chives or 1 tsp. (5 ml) ground chili powder in place of the parsley.

Use 1 small onion in place of the shallots.

Cook's Tips

Recipe can easily be adapted for an adult meal. This recipe will serve 2 adults and 1 toddler.

Useful Notes
❄: No   ❋: Yes

CHICKEN, LEEK, AND POTATO HASH

PORTIONS: Makes about 4 ❋ *PREPARATION TIME:* 10 minutes ❋ *COOKING TIME:* 30–35 minutes

A great way to use up any leftover cooked meat, this potato hash is bursting with flavor, and makes a healthy, filling family meal.

2 tbsp. (30 ml) olive oil

2 potatoes, peeled and cut into ¹/₂-inch (1-cm) cubes

2 leeks, sliced

1 small onion, chopped

1 clove garlic, crushed

6 oz. (180 g) cooked chicken, ground or very finely chopped

2 tbsp. (30 ml) chopped fresh parsley

1 Heat the oil in a large nonstick skillet. Add the potatoes, leeks, onion, and garlic and fry over medium heat for 5 minutes, stirring frequently, until the onions and leeks are softened.

2 Reduce the heat slightly and cook for 20–25 minutes longer, or until the potatoes are crispy, stirring occasionally.

3 Add the cooked chicken and chopped parsley to the pan, stir to mix, then cook for 5 minutes longer, until the chicken is piping hot, stirring frequently.

4 Serve the hash immediately with a chopped mixed garden salad and a slice of fresh crusty bread.

Variations

Use cooked beef or ham in place of the chicken.

Use 1 tbsp. (15 ml) chopped fresh rosemary in place of the parsley.

Use sweet potatoes in place of the standard potatoes.

Cook's Tips

Always clean leeks under running cold water before use to flush out any dirt from the layers.

Recipe can easily be adapted for an adult meal. This recipe will serve 1–2 adults and 1 toddler.

Nutrition Notes
Vitamin C: ▲

Useful Notes
❄: No   ❋: Yes

WILD WEST VEGETABLE CHILI TACOS

PORTIONS: Makes about 4 ❀ *PREPARATION TIME:* 10 minutes ❀ *COOKING TIME:* 30 minutes

This mild vegetable chili, served in crisp taco shells and topped with grated cheese, combines lots of delicious flavors and textures to tempt toddlers.

1 cup (250 ml) canned chopped tomatoes	1 small carrot, chopped	1 tbsp. (15 ml) tomato ketchup
³/₄ cup (350 ml) canned red kidney beans, rinsed and drained	1/2 cup (125 ml) diced, seeded red pepper	1/2 tsp. (2.5 ml) hot chili powder
¹/₂ cup (125 ml) diced rutabaga	1 clove garlic, crushed	4 taco shells
1 small onion, chopped	4 tbsp. (60 ml) unsweetened apple juice	1 tbsp. (15 ml) finely grated cheddar cheese
		1 tbsp. (15 ml) chopped fresh parsley

1 Place all the ingredients, except the taco shells, cheese, and parsley, in a saucepan and mix well.

2 Cover and bring to a boil, then simmer gently for 15 minutes, stirring occasionally. Increase the heat slightly, uncover, and simmer for 10–15 minutes longer, until the vegetables are cooked and tender and the sauce has thickened, stirring occasionally.

3 Place the taco shells on a baking sheet and bake in a preheated oven at 350°F (180°C) for 2–3 minutes, or according to the package instructions.

4 To fill the taco shells, hold a shell in one hand and spoon some filling into the shell. Sprinkle with cheese and parsley and serve immediately. Serve with homemade coleslaw and fresh bread.

Variations

Use parsnip or turnip in place of the rutabaga.

Use 1 cup (250 ml) skinned and chopped fresh tomatoes in place of the canned tomatoes.

Use curry powder in place of the chili powder.

Cook's Tips

Recipe can easily be adapted for an adult meal. This recipe will serve 1–2 adults and 1 toddler.

Do not freeze the filled taco shells.

Nutrition Notes

Calcium: ▲   *Vitamin C:* ▲▲

Useful Notes

❀: Yes   ✿: Yes, but the sauce only

TUNA LASAGNE

PORTIONS: makes about 6 ✿ *PREPARATION TIME:* 25 minutes
COOKING TIME: 35-45 minutes

Using tuna instead of traditional ground beef in this lasagne makes a flavorful change which the whole family will enjoy.

1 cup (250 ml) canned chopped tomatoes or 1 cup (250 ml) skinned and chopped fresh tomatoes

1 small onion, chopped

1 clove garlic, crushed

1 small yellow pepper, seeded and diced

1 zucchini, diced

1½ cups (375 ml) sliced mushrooms

4 tbsp. (60 ml) vegetable stock (see page 14)

7 oz. (210 g) canned tuna in water, drained and flaked

1 tsp. (5 ml) Italian seasoning

2 tbsp. (30 ml) butter or margarine

2 tbsp. (30 ml) all-purpose flour

2 cups (500 ml) milk

½ cup (125 ml) finely grated cheddar cheese

4 oz. (115 g) precooked lasagne

2 tbsp. (30 ml) finely grated cheddar cheese

1 Place all the vegetables and the vegetable stock in a large saucepan and mix thoroughly. Cover the pan and bring to a boil, then simmer gently for 10 minutes, stirring occasionally. Remove the pan from the heat and stir in the drained and flaked tuna and the Italian seasoning.

2 Meanwhile, place the butter or margarine in a saucepan with the flour and milk. Heat gently, whisking continuously, until the sauce comes to a boil and thickens. Simmer gently for 2 minutes, stirring. Remove the pan from the heat and stir in the cheddar cheese.

3 To assemble the lasagne, place half the tuna mixture over the base of a shallow, ovenproof dish or baking pan. Cover with half the pasta and top with one-third of the cheese sauce.

4 Repeat these layers, topping with the remaining sauce, to cover the pasta completely. Sprinkle the grated cheddar cheese over the top.

5 Bake in a preheated oven at 350°F (180°C) for 35–45 minutes, or until golden brown on top and bubbling. Serve with a chopped mixed salad and fresh crusty bread.

✿

Variations

Use canned salmon in place of the tuna.

Use fresh Parmesan cheese in place of the cheddar cheese for the top.

Use tarragon in place of the Italian seasoning.

✿

Cook's Tips

To skin fresh tomatoes, cut a small cross on the bottom of each tomato using a sharp knife. Place the tomatoes in a bowl of boiling water for about 12 seconds, then remove using a slotted spoon. Cool slightly, peel, and discard the skins, then chop the flesh.

Recipe can easily be adapted for an adult meal. This lasagne will serve 2 adults and 2 toddlers.

☆

Nutrition Notes

Calcium: ▲   *Vitamin C:* ▲

✎

Useful Notes

❀: No   ✿: Yes

SPINACH AND HAMBURGERS

PORTIONS: Makes 8 hamburgers ✪ *PREPARATION TIME:* 15 minutes ✪ *COOKING TIME:* 15 minutes

Adding spinach to a burger is a great way to include this nutritious vegetable in your child's diet. Hamburgers are always popular, especially if served in warm buns.

4 oz. (115 g) cooked spinach, drained

1/2 lb. (250 g) lean ground beef

1 small onion, grated or finely chopped

1/2 cup (125 ml) fresh white bread crumbs

1 tsp. (5 ml) English mustard

1 tsp. (5 ml) dried Herbes de Provence

1 tsp. (5 ml) Worcestershire sauce

1 Press any excess water out of the spinach using a wooden spoon or potato masher, then chop the spinach finely.

2 Place the cooked spinach in a bowl with all the remaining ingredients and stir thoroughly to mix.

3 Shape into 8 round flat patties and place on a broiler rack in a broiler pan.

4 Broil under a preheated medium broiler for 10–15 minutes, turning occasionally, until cooked to your liking.

5 Serve in warmed hamburger buns with a tomato and lettuce garnish, and top with a little grated cheese, if you like.

Variations
Use ground pork, chicken, or turkey in place of the beef.

Use whole-wheat bread crumbs in place of the white bread crumbs.

Use 1 small leek in place of the onion.

Cook's Tips
Brush the hamburgers lightly with oil before broiling, if you like.

Recipe can easily be adapted for an adult meal. This recipe will serve 2–3 adults and 1–2 toddlers.

Freeze the hamburgers raw before they are cooked.

Nutrition Notes
Iron: ▲

Useful Notes
❄: No   ✪: *Yes, but only the raw hamburgers*

STUFFED ZUCCHINI

PORTIONS: Makes about 4 ✿ PREPARATION TIME: 20 minutes ✿ COOKING TIME: 25–30 minutes

Stuffed vegetables, such as these, are a good way to encourage children to eat and enjoy vegetables.

2 zucchini

1 tbsp. (15 ml) sunflower oil

1 shallot, finely chopped

1 clove garlic, crushed

2 tbsp. (30 ml) finely chopped, seeded red pepper

1/3 cup (80 ml) finely chopped mushrooms

1 slice lean cooked ham, diced

2 tbsp. (30 ml) tomato juice

1 tbsp. (15 ml) tomato paste

1 tbsp. (15 ml) chopped fresh basil

1/2 cup (125 ml) grated cheddar cheese

1 Cut the zucchini in half lengthways and scoop out the flesh. Reserve the shells and chop the flesh finely.

2 Heat the oil in a saucepan, add the zucchini flesh, shallot, garlic, red pepper, mushrooms, and ham and cook for 3 minutes, stirring frequently.

3 Add the tomato juice, tomato paste and basil, stir to mix, and cook for 5 minutes longer, stirring occasionally.

4 Place the zucchini shells in a lightly greased, shallow ovenproof dish and divide the tomato mixture between them.

5 Sprinkle the grated cheese over the top of the zucchini and bake in a preheated oven at 350°F (180°C) for 25–30 minutes, or until the zucchini are cooked through and tender.

6 Serve one filled zucchini half per portion with lightly roasted or fried potato slices and a mixed leaf salad.

Variations
Use smoked ham in place of the unsmoked ham.

Use grated carrot in place of the mushrooms.

Use other hard cheese such as Monterey jack or Gruyère in place of the cheddar cheese.

Cook's Tips
Omit the ham to create a recipe suitable for vegetarians.

Recipe can easily be adapted for an adult meal. This recipe will serve 1–2 adults and 1 toddler.

Nutrition Notes
Calcium: ▲   *Vitamin C:* ▲▲

Useful Notes
❄: No   ❄: Yes

SWEET-AND-SOUR RICE SALAD

PORTIONS: Makes about 4 ❂ PREPARATION TIME: 10 minutes ❂ COOKING TIME: 5 minutes

A rice salad full of interesting flavors, combining cooked rice and chopped fresh raw vegetables.

For the sweet-and-sour sauce:

1 tsp. (5 ml) cornstarch

4 tbsp. (60 ml) unsweetened apple juice

1 tbsp. (15 ml) soy sauce

1 tbsp. (15 ml) light soft brown sugar

1 tbsp. (15 ml) tomato ketchup

1 tbsp. (15 ml) red-wine vinegar

For the rice salad:

²/₃ cup (160 ml) cooked white or brown rice

6 scallions, chopped

10 cherry tomatoes, quartered

¹/₂ cup (125 ml) diced, seeded red pepper

³/₄ cup (350 ml) drained, canned corn kernels

²/₃ cup (160 ml) sliced button mushrooms

1 To make the sauce, blend the cornstarch with the apple juice in a saucepan. Add the remaining sauce ingredients and stir until well combined.

2 Heat gently, stirring continuously, until the sauce comes to a boil and thickens slightly. Simmer gently for 2 minutes, stirring. Remove the pan from the heat and set aside while you prepare the salad.

3 Place all the rice salad ingredients in a bowl and stir to mix.

4 Pour the sweet-and-sour sauce over the rice salad and toss together to mix.

5 Serve the rice salad warm or allow to cool, cover, and chill before serving. Serve with broiled fish or chicken fingers.

Variations

Other vegetables that go well with this salad include sliced zucchini, cooked pumpkin chunks, and chopped cooked green beans.

Use cooked pasta or noodles in place of the rice.

❂

Cook's Tips

Serve the sweet-and-sour sauce with stir-fried meats, such as shredded chicken or beef, and mixed vegetables.

Recipe can easily be adapted for an adult meal. This rice salad will serve 2 adults and 1 toddler.

Nutrition Notes

Vitamin C: ▲

Useful Notes

❀: Yes ❂: Yes

MILD VEGETABLE CURRY WITH COUSCOUS

PORTIONS: Makes about 4 ❂ PREPARATION TIME: 10 minutes ❂ COOKING TIME: 25–30 minutes

A quick-and-easy dish to prepare, this recipe combines the delicate flavor of curried vegetables with the wonderful texture of couscous.

1 leek, sliced

2 shallots, chopped

1 small turnip, diced

1 small parsnip, diced

1 small carrot, diced

1 small green pepper, seeded and diced

¹/₂ cup (125 ml) small cauliflower flowerets

²/₃ cup (160 ml) sliced button mushrooms

¹/₂ cup (125 ml) frozen lima beans

³/₄ cup (180 ml) vegetable stock (see page 14)

2 tbsp. (30 ml) tomato paste

1 tsp. (5 ml) ground coriander

¹/₂ tsp. (2.5 ml) each chili powder, ground cumin, and turmeric

1 cup (250 ml) quick-cook couscous

1 Place all the ingredients, except the couscous, in a saucepan and stir to mix.

2 Cover, bring to a boil, and simmer for 25–30 minutes, until the vegetables are cooked and tender, stirring occasionally.

3 Meanwhile, soak and cook the couscous according to the package instructions.

4 Serve the vegetable curry on a bed of cooked couscous. Serve with fingers of toast, toasted pita bread, or poppadoms and homemade chutney.

Variations
Omit the spices and use 1–2 tsp. (5–10 ml)
blended curry powder.

Serve the mild vegetable curry on
a bed of boiled rice or pasta, in place of
the couscous.

Cook's Tips
Try experimenting with different flavors and spices.
Start by adding a small amount
and then increase to more adult spice levels.

Recipe can easily be adapted for an adult meal.
This curry will serve 2 adults and 1 toddler.

Nutrition Notes
Vitamin C: ▲▲

Useful Notes
❀: Yes   ❀: Yes

PEPPER, LEEK, AND POTATO FRITTATA

PORTIONS: Makes about 6 ❁ PREPARATION TIME: 10 minutes ❁ COOKING TIME: 15 minutes

This frittata offers an appealing way to serve nutritious eggs and fresh vegetables to toddlers. It's also very quick and easy to make.

1 tbsp. (15 ml) olive oil

1 small red pepper, seeded and diced

1 leek, thinly sliced

1 small zucchini, thinly sliced

generous 1 cup (250 ml) diced boiled potatoes

3 eggs

1 tbsp. (15 ml) milk

1 tsp. (5 ml) Italian seasoning

1/2 cup (125 ml) grated cheddar or Monterey jack cheese

1 Heat the oil in a nonstick skillet. Add the pepper, leek, and zucchini and cook for 5 minutes, stirring occasionally. Add the potatoes and cook for 2 minutes, stirring.

2 Beat the eggs, milk, and Italian seasoning together, then pour the egg mixture evenly over the vegetables in the pan.

3 Cook over medium heat until the eggs are firmly set and the frittata is golden brown underneath.

4 Sprinkle the cheese over the top and broil under a preheated medium broiler until the cheese has melted and the top is golden brown.

5 Serve in slices with fresh seasonal vegetables, such as cabbage or corn, and warm crusty bread.

Variations

Use boiled sweet potatoes in place of the standard potatoes.

Use dried tarragon or rosemary in place of the Italian seasoning.

Cook's Tips

The eggs should be cooked thoroughly.

Recipe can easily be adapted for an adult meal. This frittata will serve 2 adults and 2 toddlers.

Nutrition Notes

Calcium: ▲   Vitamin C: ▲

Useful Notes

❄: Yes   ❄: No

HERBY SHRIMP AND MUSHROOM PILAF

PORTIONS: Makes about 4
PREPARATION TIME: 10 minutes
COOKING TIME: 35 minutes

Combine shrimp, vegetables, and rice to add a new dimension to your toddler's eating experience.

1/2 cup (125 ml) long-grain brown rice

1 small onion, chopped

1 leek, finely chopped

1 clove garlic, crushed

1 1/2 cups (375 ml) sliced mushrooms

1 1/2 cups (375 ml) vegetable stock (see page 14)

4 oz. (115 g) cooked, shelled shrimp

3/4 cup (180 ml) frozen peas

1 tbsp. (15 ml) chopped fresh mixed herbs

1 Place the rice, onion, leek, garlic, mushrooms, and stock in a saucepan and stir. Cover, bring to a boil, and simmer for 25 minutes, stirring occasionally.

2 Stir in the shrimp and peas and simmer, uncovered, for a 5–10 minutes longer, or until the rice is cooked and tender and the pilaf is piping hot. Add a little extra stock if necessary.

3 Stir in the herbs and serve immediately with fingers of bread or toast.

❁

Cook's Tips

For a vegetarian option, omit the shrimp and add 3/4 cup (180 ml) drained, canned beans, such as red kidney beans or black-eyed peas.

Recipe can easily be adapted for an adult meal. This pilaf will serve 1–2 adults and 1 toddler.

Useful Notes

❄: No   ❄: No

CHUNKY VEGETABLE SOUP

PORTIONS: Makes about 4 ❁ *PREPARATION TIME:* 10 minutes ❁ *COOKING TIME:* 25 minutes

Soups are easy for children to eat and fun for dipping bread or toast into. The interesting texture of the diced vegetables in this soup makes it a popular choice with the grown-ups, too.

1 Heat the oil in a saucepan, add the carrot, parsnip, potato, onion, leek, and celery, and cook gently for 5 minutes, stirring occasionally.

2 Add the peas or petit pois, dried herbs, and stock and stir thoroughly to mix. Cover, bring to a boil, and cook gently for about 20 minutes, or until the vegetables are tender, stirring occasionally.

3 Serve with fingers of fresh crusty bread or toast, or fun-shaped bread croutons. Sprinkle with a little grated cheese just before serving, if you like.

❁
Cook's Tips

For a smooth-textured soup, the cooked soup can be cooled slightly, then puréed and reheated before serving.

Recipe can easily be adapted for an adult meal. This soup will serve 1–2 adults and 1 toddler. Serve the adult portion with warm ciabatta rolls or wedges of foccacia bread.

✎
Useful Notes
❀: *Yes* ❁: *Yes*

2 tsp. (10 ml) sunflower oil	*1 small leek, sliced*
1 small carrot, diced	*1 stick celery, finely chopped*
1 small parsnip, diced	*¹/₂ cup (125 ml) frozen peas or petit pois*
1 small potato, diced	*1 tsp. (5 ml) dried Herbes de Provence*
1 small onion, chopped	*1¹/₄ cups (310 ml) vegetable stock (see page 14)*

BAKED POTATO, BREAD, OR TOAST TOPPERS

PORTIONS: Each topping generously tops one medium baked potato, or one slice of bread or toast. ✪ *PREPARATION TIME:* 10 minutes
COOKING TIME: About 1 hour (for baked potato)

Baked potatoes, bread, and toast are three staple foods which can be enjoyed all year round, at any main or snack meal. We've suggested some quick-and-easy recipe ideas for toppings for either a baked potato, a slice of bread, or a slice of toast, to fill a hungry child.

TO BAKE A POTATO

Wash, dry, and prick the potato with a fork. Bake in a preheated oven at 400°F (200°C) for 1–1½ hours, until cooked and tender. Cut a cross in the top of the potato or cut it in half and serve with one of the following delicious toppings.

EGG AND TOMATO

1 small egg, hard-boiled and shelled

1 tomato, chopped

2 tsp. (10 ml) mayonnaise

2 tsp. (10 ml) chopped fresh chives or parsley

Mash the egg, add the tomato, mayonnaise, and chives or parsley and mix well. Replace 1 tsp. (5 ml) mayonnaise with plain yogurt for a lower fat option, or serve without the mayonnaise if you prefer. Spoon onto a baked potato, or spread onto a slice of bread or toast.

☆
Nutrition Notes
Vitamin C: ▲

✎
Useful Notes
❀: *Yes* ❄: *No*

CHEESE AND CARROT

3 tbsp. (45 ml) grated cheddar cheese

2 tbsp. (30 ml) grated carrot

1 tbsp. (15 ml) raisins

Mix together the ingredients. Spoon onto a baked potato, or spread onto a slice of bread or toast.

☆
Nutrition Notes
Calcium: ▲▲

✎
Useful Notes
❀: *Yes* ❄: *No*

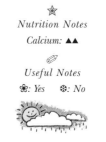

TUNA AND CORN

4 tbsp. (60 ml) drained and flaked canned tuna

½ cup (125 ml) drained canned corn kernels

2 tsp. (10 ml) mayonnaise

1 tsp. (5 ml) whole-milk plain yogurt

2 tsp. (10 ml) chopped fresh chives

Mix together and spoon onto a baked potato, or spread onto bread or toast.

✎
Useful Notes
❀: *No* ❄: *No*

SMOKED HAM AND TOMATO

1 tomato, chopped

2 tbsp. (30 ml) diced lean cooked smoked ham

2 scallions, chopped

2 tsp. (10 ml) tomato ketchup or chutney

Mix together and spoon onto a baked potato, or spread onto bread or toast.

☆
Nutrition Notes
Vitamin C: ▲

✎
Useful Notes
❀: *No* ❄: *No*

APRICOT COLESLAW

3 tbsp. (45 ml) grated carrot

½ cup (125 ml) shredded cabbage

2 tbsp. (30 ml) chopped ready-to-eat dried apricots

2 tsp. (10 ml) mayonnaise

1 tsp. (5 ml) whole-milk plain yogurt

Mix together and spoon onto a baked potato, or spread onto bread or toast.

☆
Nutrition Notes
Iron: ▲   *Vitamin C:* ▲

✎
Useful Notes
❀: *Yes* ❄: *No*

PEAR-CHOCOLATE UPSIDE-DOWN PUDDING

PORTIONS: Makes about 6 ❂ *PREPARATION TIME:* 15 minutes ❂ *COOKING TIME:* 35–40 minutes

No apologies for this delicious chocolate treat for toddlers, children, and adults alike!
A layer of juicy pears served with a light chocolate cake, topped with chocolate custard sauce, is a
winning combination of flavors—and it's easy to make.

For the pudding:

2 tbsp. (30 ml) golden or corn syrup

¹/₂ lb. (250 g) canned pear quarters in fruit juice, drained

4 tbsp. (60 ml) butter or margarine

¹/₄ cup (60 ml) sugar

1 egg, beaten

¹/₂ cup (125 ml) self-rising flour, sifted

1 tbsp. (15 ml) unsweetened cocoa powder, sifted

¹/₂ tsp. (2.5 ml) baking powder, sifted

1 tbsp. (15 ml) milk

For the chocolate custard sauce:

1 tbsp. (15 ml) cornstarch

2 tsp. (10 ml) unsweetened cocoa powder

2 tsp. (10 ml) sugar

³/₄ cup (180 ml) plus 2 tbsp. (30 ml) milk

1 To make the sponge pudding, place the syrup in a small saucepan and heat gently until it becomes more liquid. Pour over the base of a lightly greased 6-inch (15-cm) deep, round ovenproof soufflé dish.

2 Arrange the pear quarters, cut side up, in the syrup over the base of the dish.

3 Place the butter or margarine, sugar, beaten egg, flour, cocoa powder, baking powder, and milk in a bowl and beat thoroughly using an electric mixer or a wooden spoon, until the mixture is smooth and well blended.

4 Spoon the pudding batter over the pears and level the surface with the back of the spoon. Bake in a preheated oven at 350°F (180°C) for 35–40 minutes, or until the pudding is well risen and springy to the touch.

5 Meanwhile, make the chocolate custard sauce. Place the custard powder, cocoa powder, and sugar in a small bowl. Add a little milk and mix thoroughly to make a smooth paste.

6 Heat the remaining milk in a small saucepan until almost boiling. Pour the hot milk onto the blended custard mixture, stirring continuously.

7 Return the mixture to the pan and heat gently, stirring continuously, until the custard sauce comes to a boil and thickens. Simmer the sauce gently for 1 minute, stirring continuously.

8 Turn the baked pudding out onto a warmed serving plate. Cut into generous wedges and serve with the chocolate custard sauce alongside or poured over.

Variations

Look for golden syrup in gourmet food stores, where it is imported from Britain. Corn syrup can be used as a substitute, although it has a milder flavor.

Use light soft brown sugar in place of the white sugar.

Cook's Tips

Recipe can easily be adapted for an adult meal. This pudding will serve 2 adults and 2 toddlers.

Nutrition Notes

Calcium: ▲

Useful Notes

❄: Yes   ✿: Yes

BANANA CHEESECAKE

PORTIONS: Makes about 6 ❋ *PREPARATION TIME:* 25 minutes plus chilling time

Bananas are one of the most versatile and nutritious fruits available. This creamy banana cheesecake is a taste-bud delight for toddlers who love bananas.

4 tbsp. (60 ml) butter or margarine

1 cup (250 ml) crushed graham cracker crumbs

2 tsp. (10 ml) unflavored gelatin

2 bananas

finely grated peel and juice of ¹/₂ lemon

10 tbsp. (150 ml) light cream cheese

²/₃ cup (160 ml) whole-milk plain yogurt

2 tbsp. (30 ml) sugar

banana slices brushed with a little lemon juice, to decorate

1 Melt the butter or margarine in a saucepan, add the cracker crumbs, and mix well. Press evenly over the base of a loose-bottomed 6-inch (15-cm) cake pan. Chill in the refrigerator for 30 minutes.

2 Sprinkle the gelatin over 2 tbsp. (30 ml) water in a small bowl and leave to soak for a few minutes. Place the bowl over a pan of simmering water and stir continuously until the gelatin has dissolved completely. Set aside to cool.

3 Peel and mash the bananas with the lemon peel and juice. Place the mashed bananas, cream cheese, yogurt, and sugar in a blender or food processor and blend until smooth and thoroughly mixed. Add the cooled gelatin liquid to the mixture and blend until well mixed.

4 Pour the banana mixture over the cracker base and level the surface. Chill in the refrigerator for several hours or overnight, until completely set.

5 Carefully remove the cheesecake from the tin and place it on a serving plate. Decorate with banana slices brushed with a little lemon juice just before serving.

Variations

Use other mashed fruit, such as strawberries or apricots, in place of the bananas.

Add ¹/₂ tsp. (2.5 ml) apple spice mix or ginger to the cracker base mixture.

Cook's Tips

Toss peeled and prepared bananas in a little lemon juice or brush them with a little lemon juice to prevent the bananas discoloring.

Recipe can easily be adapted for an adult meal. This cheesecake will serve 2 adults and 2 toddlers. Serve the adult portions with extra fresh fruit, if you like.

Useful Notes

❄: No   ✿: No

To make suitable for vegetarians, use a vegetarian gelatin-equivalent product, such as agar-agar.

BAKED FRUIT BONANZA

PORTIONS: Makes about 3 ❁ *PREPARATION TIME:* 10 minutes ❁ *COOKING TIME:* 30 minutes

A selection of sliced fruits lightly baked in a little fruit juice makes a simple, nutritious dessert which can be enjoyed by the whole family. It is particularly good served with yogurt or ice cream.

1 eating apple

1 pear

1 nectarine or peach

1 banana

2 tbsp. (30 ml) unsweetened apple juice

2 tbsp. (30 ml) unsweetened orange juice

1/2 tsp. (2.5 ml) apple spice mix

1 Peel, core, and slice the apple and pear. Place in a shallow, ovenproof dish.

2 Peel, pit, and slice the nectarine or peach, peel and slice the banana, and add to the dish. Toss the fruit together to mix.

3 Mix together the fruit juices and spice and pour over the fruit.

4 Cover the dish with foil and bake in a preheated oven at 350°F (180°C) for about 30 minutes, or until the fruit is softened, stirring occasionally.

❁
Cook's Tips

For a special treat, drizzle a little honey over the fruit before baking it.

Recipe can easily be adapted for an adult meal. This dessert will serve 1 adult and 1 toddler.

✦
Nutrition Notes
Vitamin C: ▲

✐
Useful Notes
❁: *Yes*   ❁: *No*

HOT LEMON SOUFFLÉ

PORTIONS: Makes about 6 ❁ *PREPARATION TIME:* 15 minutes ❁ *COOKING TIME:* 30–45 minutes

This light dessert is best served hot, but any leftovers nevertheless make a delicious treat when cold.

1 tbsp. (15 ml) butter or margarine

1 tbsp. (15 ml) all-purpose flour

1/2 cup (125 ml) milk

finely grated peel and juice of 1/2 small lemon

2 eggs, separated, plus 1 extra egg white

2 tbsp. (30 ml) sugar

sifted confectioners' sugar, to dust (optional)

1 Lightly grease a 3½-cup (875 ml) soufflé dish and set aside.

2 Place the butter or margarine, flour, and milk in a saucepan and heat gently, whisking continuously, until the sauce comes to a boil and thickens. Simmer gently for 2 minutes, stirring.

3 Stir the lemon peel and juice into the mixture, then beat in the egg yolks and sugar, mixing well.

4 Whisk the egg whites until stiff, then fold them carefully into the lemon mixture using a large metal spoon, being careful not to overmix.

5 Spoon the egg-and-lemon mixture into the prepared soufflé dish, then bake in a preheated oven at 350°F (180°C) for 30–45 minutes, or until well risen and golden brown on top.

6 Dust with sifted confectioners' sugar, if you like, and serve immediately.

Variations

Use the finely grated peel and juice of 1 lime or 1 small orange in place of the lemon.

Omit the lemon peel and use a few drops of vanilla extract for a vanilla soufflé.

❁
Cook's Tips

Recipe can easily be adapted for an adult meal. This dessert will serve 2 adults and 1 toddler. Serve the adult portions with fresh fruit, such as strawberries, if you like.

Cool, cover, and keep in the refrigerator for up to 1 day.

✐
Useful Notes
❁: *Yes*   ❁: *No*

SUMMER FRUIT SALAD

PORTIONS: Makes about 6 ☀ *PREPARATION TIME:* 15 minutes

A colorful combination of chopped fresh fruits makes a light, refreshing dessert for a warm summer's day.

¹/₃ cup (80 ml) peeled, seeded, and diced melon

¹/₃ cup (80 ml) halved seedless grapes

1 orange, peeled and segmented

1 kiwi fruit, peeled and chopped

1 eating apple, cored and chopped

¹/₃ cup (80 ml) halved or chopped strawberries

¹/₃ cup (80 ml) raspberries

4 fresh dates, pitted and chopped

¹/₂ (125 ml) unsweetened apple juice

¹/₂ (125 ml) unsweetened pineapple juice

1 Place all the prepared fruit in a bowl and stir gently to mix.

2 Mix together the fruit juices and pour over the fruit. Stir gently to mix.

3 Cover and set aside to stand for a couple of hours before serving, to allow the flavors to blend. Alternatively, cover and chill before serving.

4 Serve with whole-milk plain yogurt, or frozen yogurt.

Variations

Use your own selection of fresh fruits in season, or mix prepared fresh fruits with fruits canned in fruit juice.

Use other unsweetened fruit juices, such as orange or tropical fruit juice, in place of the apple and pineapple juices.

Cook's Tips

Recipe can easily be adapted for an adult meal. This fruit salad will serve 2 adults and 2 toddlers.

Nutrition Notes

Vitamin C: ▲▲

Useful Notes

☀: *Yes* ☀: *No*

BANANA TEA LOAF

PORTIONS: Makes 8–10 slices ✿ *PREPARATION TIME:* 15 minutes ✿ *COOKING TIME:* 45–60 minutes

*A slice of this fruity tea loaf makes a healthy midmorning or afternoon snack,
to keep an energetic toddler content.*

4 tbsp. (60 ml) butter or soft margarine

4 tbsp. (60 ml) sugar

1 egg, beaten

³/₄ cup (180 ml) sifted self-rising white flour

1 tsp (5 ml) baking powder

1 tsp (5 ml) ground ginger

2 bananas, peeled and mashed with a little lemon juice

¹/₂ cup (125 ml) finely chopped ready-to-eat dried apricots

1 Place all the ingredients, except the apricots, in a bowl. Beat thoroughly, using an electric mixer or wooden spoon, until smooth and thoroughly mixed. Stir in the apricots and mix well.

2 Turn the mixture into a lightly greased 8¹/₂ x 4¹/₂ inch (21.5 x 11.25 cm) bread pan and level.

3 Bake in a preheated oven at 350°F (180°C) for 45–60 minutes, or until well risen, golden brown, and firm to the touch.

4 Allow to cool in the pan for a couple of minutes, then turn out on to a wire rack to cool completely.

5 Serve warm or cold in slices, or cut into fingers. For a special treat, spread with butter or margarine, jam, or honey.

Variations

Use golden raisins or other chopped ready-to-eat dried fruit, such as pears or peaches, in place of the apricots.

Use apple pie spice or nutmeg in place of the ginger.

Use light soft brown sugar in place of the white sugar.

Cook's Tips

A quick-and-easy way to chop dried fruit such as apricots is to snip them into pieces using a pair of clean kitchen scissors.

Useful Notes

: Yes ✿: Yes

CARROT AND GOLDEN RAISIN FINGERS

PORTIONS: Makes 10 fingers ✿ PREPARATION TIME: 10 minutes ✿ COOKING TIME: 30–35 minutes

Full of delicious flavor, these moist finger cakes make an ideal afternoon snack or treat.

6 tbsp. (90 ml) butter or margarine

6 tbsp. (90 ml) light soft brown sugar

1 egg, beaten

¾ cup (180 ml) coarsely grated carrots

⅔ cup (160 ml) self-rising flour, sifted

½ cup (125 ml) golden raisins

1 tsp. (5 ml) finely grated orange peel (optional)

1 Cream the butter or margarine and sugar together until light and fluffy, then add the beaten egg, a little at a time, beating well after each addition.

2 Fold in the carrots, flour, golden raisins, and peel, if using. Mix well.

3 Turn the mixture into a lightly greased 6-inch (15-cm) shallow, square cake pan and level the surface.

4 Bake in a preheated oven at 350°F (180°C) for 30–35 minutes, or until risen and golden brown.

5 Cool slightly, then mark into fingers using a sharp knife. Allow to cool completely in the pan, then cut into fingers to serve.

Variations

Use grated zucchini in place of the carrots.

Use raisins or chopped ready-to-eat dried apricots in place of the golden raisins.

Use grated lemon peel in place of the orange.

✿

Cook's Tips

Once cool, wrap in foil or store in an airtight container.

✎

General Notes

❄: Yes ✿: Yes

APPLE AND APRICOT CRUMBLE

PORTIONS: Makes about 4 ✿ PREPARATION TIME: 10 minutes ✿ COOKING TIME: 35–45 minutes

Variations

Use porridge oats in place of the oatmeal.

Use apple pie spice or ginger in place of the cinnamon.

Use other mixtures of fruit, such as pears and peaches, in place of the apples and apricots.

Cook's Tips

Recipe can easily be adapted for an adult meal. It will serve 1–2 adults and 1 toddler.

✦

Nutrition Notes

We have used eating apples which are naturally sweet and apricots canned in fruit juice for this crumble, so there is no need to add extra sugar to sweeten the fruit.

Vitamin C: ▲

Useful Notes

❄: Yes ✿: Yes

Fruit crumbles make a substantial, nutritious dessert. Here we've included oatmeal for a change, to make a crispy topping.

2 tbsp. (30 ml) all-purpose flour

⅓ cup (80 ml) quick-cooking oatmeal

2 tbsp. (30 ml) butter or margarine, diced

2 tbsp. (30 ml) light soft brown sugar

½ tsp. (2.5 ml) ground cinnamon

2 eating apples

1 cup (125 ml) canned apricot halves in fruit juice

1 Place the flour and oatmeal in a bowl and stir to mix. Cut in the butter or margarine, then stir in the sugar and cinnamon and mix well.

2 Peel, core, and thinly slice the apples and place in the base of an ovenproof dish. Stir in the apricots and apricot juice.

3 Sprinkle the crumble mixture over the fruit, pressing it down lightly.

4 Bake in a preheated oven at 350°F (180°C) for 35–45 minutes, or until the fruit is cooked and the crumble is lightly browned. Serve the crumble hot or cold, either with yogurt or ice cream.

CHAPTER 5
1–5 YEARS

toDDLeR PaRties aND PicNics

Toddler parties and picnics can provide the opportunity for children and adults—friends and family— to have a great time together. If your baby's birthday falls in a summer month, why not plan a picnic with a small group of friends, preparing food and drink which will appeal to babies and adults alike—in much the same way that you plan your everyday meals.

Indoor parties for slightly older children offer plenty of scope for enjoyment, both in preparation for the event and on the day. If you are feeling ambitious and creative, develop a fun theme for the occasion, and style party wear, table settings, food, and games to coordinate.

HAVING FUN WITH FOOD

The age of your baby or child will partly determine the nature and focus of your party or picnic. For your baby's first and second birthdays, you will probably be catering more for the grown-ups than the babies, since they may be too young to appreciate the celebration. When your child is a little older, from around 3 onward, she will begin to really look forward to parties and picnics, and you can introduce simple games and activities.

Sitting down to enjoy party food is an important part of the celebration, so it's worth taking the time to plan ahead. You might like to think about the following:

- presentation—not only how the food will look on the table, but also the table cloth, plates, and napkins
- the type of food to serve and how
- drinks
- accessories, such as party hats, streamers, and so on

Presentation: Setting the scene

The table and the food presented on it has to look inviting, so think about a color scheme or perhaps a theme for the party. A plastic cloth is great for the inevitable spillages, but you can also buy brightly colored paper cloths, with matching napkins, or you might like to use a combination of both!

Paper plates and cups are available in an array of colors, sizes, and themes, and are more practical than using your own (they also make clearing up easier). You might like to think about other table accessories, such as streamers, party hats, and balloons—anything which will have a visual impact as the children sit down to eat. It's worth remembering, though, that too many accessories can sometimes be a distraction, and you might find that the children are more interested in the party hats than your food!

Party food

We've developed a selection of ideas for toddler party food for you to pick and

choose from. It's worth remembering that toddlers may not eat that much at parties, so don't spend hours preparing a wonderful spread, unless you have other family members ready and willing to eat up the leftovers! Choose four or five different savory items and perhaps two or three sweet dishes. Have the savory dishes in place on the table when the children sit down, so that they have something to tuck into straight away.

Some example combinations might be:

Savory
A variety of Pinwheel and Zebra Sandwiches *(pages 110–111, but see Picnics, page 105 for more filling ideas)*
Chicken and Sesame Fingers *(page 107)*
Fun Pizza Faces *(page 106)*
Cheese Twists *(page 109)*

Sweet
Mini-Chocolate Chip Muffins *(page 118)*
Fruity Oatmeal Squares *(page 120)*
Mixed Berry Milk Molds *(page 114)*

OR
Savory
A variety of Pinwheel and Zebra Sandwiches *(pages 110–111)*
Tuna and Avocado Pasta Salad *(page 108)*
Campfire Sausage Kabobs *(page 113)*
Cheese Twists *(page 109)*

Sweet
Apple and Spice Bars *(page 119)*
Mini-Chocolate Chip Muffins *(page 118)*
Frozen Raspberry Yogurt *(page 114)*

In addition to the recipes we've suggested, why not also serve some of the following "nibbles" for a variety of tastes, textures, and colors:

- cherry tomatoes
- seedless green and black grapes, cut in half
- small cubes of hard cheese, or grated hard cheese
- vegetable sticks (carrot sticks, red and yellow peppers, cucumber batons, celery sticks, radishes), and breadsticks with a savory dip
- platter of exotic fruit slices (mango, kiwi fruit, pineapple, and so on)

Some of the above foods also make attractive garnishes. Other garnishes include: thin slices of cucumber, scallion fans, radish flowers, and sprigs of fresh herbs or herb leaves and flowers.

Children love animal shapes, so why not use cookie cutters to make different shapes, and use foods to create faces, such as raisins for eyes, strips of tomato for a mouth, and pieces of pepper for a nose or ears. Look out for novelty animal- or character-shaped molds in stores or mail-order catalogs as a fun way to serve desserts (see page 114 for a recipe).

Drinks

Try some of these great-tasting ideas for party drinks:

- Fruit Juice Punch: Combine unsweetened orange, pineapple, and apple juices
- Fizzy Punch: Unsweetened fruit juice, such as orange, and lemonade; or orange and pineapple juice with lemonade
- Yogurt Shake: Blend plain yogurt or low-fat fruit yogurt, or both, with fresh or canned fruit—for example raspberry yogurt, plain yogurt, and fresh or canned peaches
- Ice Cream Soda: Soda water and fruit juice topped with ice cream. Try apricots, orange juice, soda water, and ice cream or frozen yogurt
- Fruit Crush/Slush: Puréed fruit and fruit juice served with crushed ice. Try puréed pineapple and juice with ice, or a mixture of pineapple and orange juice with ice
- Milk Shake (see page 121 for recipe) or Milk Shake Float: Milk shake topped with ice cream or frozen yogurt. Try strawberry milk shake topped with vanilla ice cream

Serve fruity drinks, such as punch, with fresh fruit slices, and use animal-shaped ice-cube blocks for fun, or fruit juice ice blocks for color and extra flavor. Curly straws are fun to drink from, and look attractive, too. You can serve these drinks in one of the many types of plastic or paper cups available, such as novelty ones, or character or theme cups, or ones with a curly straw attached—the list of possibilities is endless!

Birthday cakes

Birthday parties are not complete without a celebration cake with candles. Instead of the "traditional" cake, why not try an iced Carrot Cake, Madeira Cake, or Marble Cake (chocolate and vanilla), or a Banana Cake or Honey Cake. Try making a birthday cake in an unusual shape, letter, or a favorite children's character, for example, a clown.

PICNICS

A little forward planning goes a long way when it comes to creating an enjoyable picnic—cooking and freezing foods in advance saves time on the day and makes for a more relaxed mood. Take foods which will travel well, for example, sandwiches and rolls (see below for filling ideas), and baked goods such as Fruity Oatmeal Squares and Mini-Apricot Biscuits (page 120), and Mini-Chocolate Chip Muffins and Apple and Spice Bars (pages 118-119). Remember to pack lots of drinks in hot weather (see the ideas listed on the left), and refreshing fresh fruit, such as summer fruits or other fruit in season.

Fillers or toppers for sandwiches

The ingredients listed below can be used as:
- fillers for all types of breads (whole-wheat, mixed-grain, white, pita bread, bagels, fruit bread, or muffins)
- toppers for open sandwiches, crackers, or mini sandwiches

smooth peanut butter • egg and tomato • chicken and celery • tuna and cucumber • beef and watercress • cream cheese and apricot • ham and tomato • cheese and chutney • chicken and pineapple • egg and lettuce • carrot and soft cheese • tuna and pepper • banana and cream cheese • cottage cheese, pineapple, and dates • ham with cucumber relish

Tips for picnic planning

- Prepare as many dishes as possible a day in advance, then wrap and refrigerate overnight.
- Sandwiches are much better made fresh on the morning of the picnic.
- Plastic containers with tight-fitting lids are ideal for transporting foods.
- Foil and plastic wrap are useful for wrapping sandwiches and baked goods.
- Plastic food bags with twist ties are good for keeping some foods fresh.
- Vacuum flasks are excellent for keeping drinks cold or hot.
- To keep foods fresh and cold, it's best to use a cool box or an insulated picnic bag with ice packs. It's particularly important that food being served to toddlers or young children is kept fresh and cold, to prevent bacterial contamination, especially in hot weather.

FUN PIZZA FACES

PORTIONS: Makes 8 pizza faces ❁ *PREPARATION TIME:* 25 minutes ❁ *COOKING TIME:* 15–20 minutes

Children love pizzas, particularly when they look fun, too. Make a batch of these pizzas in advance and freeze them ready to throw a party or picnic.

2 tsp. (10 ml) olive oil

1 small onion, finely chopped

1 clove garlic, crushed

1 small red pepper, seeded, and finely chopped

1 tomato, skinned, seeded, and finely chopped

³/₄ cups (180 ml) self-rising white flour

³/₄ cup (180 ml) wholemeal flour

¹/₂ teaspoon (2.5 ml) baking powder

pinch of salt

4 tbsp. (60 ml) butter or margarine

about ²/₃ cup (160 ml) milk

1 tbsp. (15 ml) tomato paste

1 tbsp. (15 ml) tomato ketchup

2 tsp. (10 ml) dried Herbes de Provence

¹/₂ cup (125 ml) finely grated cheddar cheese

¹/₂ cup (125 ml) grated mozzarella cheese

8 small button mushrooms, halved and blanched

8 small broccoli flowerets, blanched

8 thin strips seeded yellow pepper, blanched

1 Heat the oil in a saucepan, add the onion, garlic, and pepper and cook for 5 minutes, stirring occasionally. Stir in the tomato, then set the pan aside while you prepare the pizza crust.

2 Place the flours, baking powder, and salt in a bowl. Cut in the butter or margarine until the mixture resembles fine bread crumbs. Add enough milk, mixing to make a soft dough, and knead lightly.

3 Divide the dough into 8 pieces and pat out or roll out into 4-inch (10-cm) circles. Place the dough circles on 2 lightly greased baking sheets, making the edges of the circles slightly thicker than the centers.

4 Mix together the tomato paste, tomato ketchup, and herbs and spread a little over each pizza crust. Spoon the onion mixture over the top.

5 Mix the 2 cheeses together and sprinkle over the pizzas. Top each pizza with the blanched vegetables arranged in the form of a fun face, for example 2 mushroom halves for eyes, a broccoli floweret for a nose, and a strip of red or yellow pepper for a mouth.

6 Bake the pizzas in a preheated oven at 400°F (200°C) for 15–20 minutes, or until risen and golden brown on top. Serve hot or cold.

Variations

Use all white flour in place of the mixture of white and whole-wheat flour.

Use your own choice of blanched vegetables to make the pizza faces.

Cook's Tips

To make a meal, serve with baked potatoes and fresh seasonal vegetables, such as cauliflower or broccoli.

Toddlers may enjoy helping Mom or Dad to make these pizzas by placing the vegetables on the pizzas to make the faces.

Make one large 10-inch (25-cm) pizza and cut into small wedges once cooked, if preferred. Bake the large pizza for 25–30 minutes.

Nutrition Notes

Calcium: ▲   Vitamin C: ▲

Useful Notes

❀: Yes   ✺: Yes

CHICKEN AND SESAME NUGGETS

PORTIONS: Makes about 8   ❂   *PREPARATION TIME:* 15 minutes   ❂   *COOKING TIME:* 20 minutes

Always a popular choice with children, these savory nuggets make a quick-and-easy party dish. Serve with different flavored dips for extra appeal and variety.

1 lb. (500 g) skinless, boneless chicken breast halves

2 eggs

2 cups (500 ml) fine whole-wheat bread crumbs

3 tbsp. (45 ml) sesame seeds

3 tbsp. (45 ml) chopped fresh mixed herbs

2 tbsp. (30 ml) all-purpose flour

1 Cut the chicken into 1-inch (2.5-cm) cubes and set aside. Beat the eggs with 2 tbsp. (30 ml) water. Mix together the bread crumbs, sesame seeds, and herbs.

2 Dip the chicken cubes firstly in the flour, then the beaten egg mixture, and finally the bread crumb mixture, ensuring that each piece of chicken is well coated all over.

3 Place the chicken nuggets on a lightly greased baking sheet and bake in a preheated oven at 400°F (200°C) for

about 20 minutes, or until cooked, golden brown, and crispy.

4 Serve hot or cold with a variety of dips, such as sweet and sour, barbecue, and spicy tomato.

Variations

Use turkey breast in place of the chicken.

Use white bread crumbs in place of the whole-wheat bread crumbs.

Use 1 tbsp. (15 ml) Italian seasoning in place of the fresh herbs.

Cook's Tips

To make a meal, serve with mashed potatoes, peas or corn, and tomato sauce or relish.

Nutrition Notes

Iron: ▲

Useful Notes

❀: No   ✺: Yes

TUNA AND AVOCADO PASTA SALAD

PORTIONS: Makes about 12 ❀ *PREPARATION TIME:* 10 minutes ❀ *COOKING TIME:* 10–12 minutes

This nutritious creamy combination of whole-wheat pasta, tuna, avocado, and vegetables, tossed together in a light mayonnaise dressing, is an ideal party or picnic dish.

1¹/₂ cups (375 ml) whole-wheat pasta shapes

2 tbsp. (30 ml) mayonnaise

2 tbsp. (30 ml) whole-milk plain yogurt

2 tbsp. (30 ml) chopped fresh mixed herbs

7 oz. (210 g) canned tuna in water,
drained and flaked

1¹/₃ cups (330 ml) drained canned corn kernels

1 red pepper, seeded and diced

1 bunch scallions, chopped

1 avocado, peeled, seed, diced, and tossed in a
little lemon juice

¹/₂ lb. (250 g) cherry tomatoes, halved

half a cucumber, diced

1 Cook the pasta shapes in a large saucepan of boiling water for 10–12 minutes, or until cooked and tender. Drain, then rinse under cold running water until cool, and drain again.

2 Place the cooked cold pasta in a large bowl. Mix together the mayonnaise, yogurt, and herbs, add to the pasta, and stir to coat the pasta all over.

3 Add the remaining ingredients and toss together to mix well. Serve immediately or cover and chill until ready to serve.

Variations

Use canned salmon in place of the tuna.

Use canned red kidney beans or fava beans in place of the corn.

Use 1 large dessert apple in place of the avocado.

❀

Cook's Tips

Once avocado has been peeled and sliced or chopped, always brush it lightly with lemon juice or vinegar to prevent discoloration.

☆

Nutrition Notes

Vitamin C: ▲

✐

Useful Notes
❀: *No* ❀: *No*

CHEESE TWISTS

PORTIONS: Makes about 24 twists ✪ *PREPARATION TIME:* 15 minutes ✪ *COOKING TIME:* 12–15 minutes

These crisp cheese pastry twists are quick to make. Children as well as adults will love to nibble on them!

²/₃ *cup (160 ml) all-purpose flour*

3 tbsp. (45 ml) butter or margarine

¹/₂ *cup (125 ml) finely grated Gruyère cheese*

¹/₂ *tsp. (2.5 ml) mustard powder*

1 egg, beaten

1 Sift the flour into a bowl and lightly cut in the butter or margarine until the mixture resembles fine bread crumbs.

2 Stir in the cheese and mustard, then add enough beaten egg to form a soft dough. Knead gently until smooth.

3 Roll the dough out on a lightly floured surface to form a rectangle about 16 x 5 inches (40 x 12.5 cm).

4 Lightly brush the dough all over with the remaining beaten egg, if you like. Cut the dough into thin rectangular strips about ¹/₂ inch (1 cm) wide, then twist the dough pieces and place them firmly in position on a lightly greased baking sheet.

5 Bake the cheese twists in a preheated oven at 350°F (180°C) for 12–15 minutes, or until golden brown. Carefully transfer the pastry twists to a wire rack to cool, then serve warm or cold.

Variations

Use a mixture of white and whole-wheat flour in place of all white flour.

For extra flavor and crunch, sprinkle the unbaked twists with sesame or poppy seeds.

✪
Cook's Tips

To make flat cheese straws, do not twist the straws before baking.

☆
Nutrition Notes

Calcium: ▲▲

Useful Notes

 : Yes   ✪: Yes

CHEESE AND HAM WHIRLS

PORTIONS: Makes about 14 whirls ❁ PREPARATION TIME: 15 minutes ❁ COOKING TIME: 10–15 minutes

It's a good idea to make up a batch of these attractive biscuit whirls in advance and freeze them.

1½ cups (375 g) self-rising flour

1 tsp. (5 ml) baking powder

pinch of salt

1 tsp. (5 ml) mustard powder

4 tbsp. (60 ml) butter or margarine

about ⅔ cup (160 ml) milk

¾ cup (180 ml) grated cheddar cheese

¾ cup (180 ml) diced cooked lean ham

3 tbsp. (45 ml) chopped fresh chives

1 Sift the flour, baking powder, salt, and mustard powder into a bowl. Lightly cut in the butter or margarine until the mixture resembles fine bread crumbs.

2 Make a well in the center and stir in enough milk to make a soft dough.

3 Turn the dough out onto a lightly floured surface. Knead gently and roll out lightly to a form a rectangle measuring about 9 x12 inches (23 x 30 cm).

4 Mix together the cheese, ham, and chives and sprinkle over the dough. From a long side, roll the dough up firmly like a jelly roll, then cut into about 14 slices.

5 Place the slices on a lightly greased baking sheet and bake in a preheated oven at 425°F (220°C) for 10–15 minutes, or until risen and golden brown.

6 Transfer to a wire rack to cool and serve warm or cold.

Variations

Use half whole-wheat and half white flours.
Use smoked ham or canned, flaked tuna in place of the unsmoked ham.

❁
Cook's Tips

To make a meal, serve the freshly baked warm biscuit whirls with baked potatoes and homemade coleslaw.

Nutrition Notes
Calcium: ▲▲

Useful Notes
❄: No ❁: Yes

PINWHEEL AND ZEBRA SANDWICHES

PORTIONS: Makes about 24 pinwheel sandwiches and 12 zebra sandwiches ❁ PREPARATION TIME: 15 minutes plus chilling time

Try these quick-and-easy pinwheel and zebra sandwiches as an attractive way to serve sandwiches.

For the pinwheel sandwiches:

4 slices medium-sliced bread, crusts removed

3 tbsp. (45 ml) light cream cheese

4 thin slices lean cooked smoked ham

1 Lay the slices of bread out on a chopping board. Roll over them lightly with a rolling pin, then spread each slice of bread with some of the cream cheese and top with a slice of the smoked ham.

2 Starting from a long side of the bread, roll up firmly like a jelly roll, then wrap in foil and chill for 1 hour. Cut each roll into about 6 slices before serving.

Variations

Use thin slices of smoked turkey, chicken, or unsmoked ham in place of the smoked ham.
Use herb-flavored cream cheese in place of the plain cream cheese.

For the zebra sandwiches:

2 slices each medium-sliced white and whole-wheat breads, crusts removed

butter or margarine, for spreading

2 tbsp. (30 ml) strawberry jam

1 banana, mashed with a little lemon juice

1 Spread both slices of white bread with a little butter or margarine, then spread with the strawberry jam.

2 Place one slice of white bread, jam side up, on a chopping board. Place one slice of whole-wheat bread on top and spread with half the mashed banana.

3 Top with the second slice of white bread, jam side up. Spread the remaining mashed banana over the jam and top with the second slice of whole-wheat bread, pressing down lightly to make the sandwich firm.

4 Cut into small squares to serve and serve immediately.

Variations

Use smooth peanut butter instead of the strawberry jam.

Use cookie cutter shapes to cut the sandwiches, for extra appeal.

Useful Notes

Pinwheel Sandwiches

❀: No   ❀: No

Zebra Sandwiches

❀: Yes   ❀: No

MEDITERRANEAN VEGETABLE BUNDLES

PORTIONS: Makes 12 bundles ✿ *PREPARATION TIME:* 25 minutes ✿ *COOKING TIME:* 20–30 minutes

A great way to serve a mixture of fresh vegetables to children. These party-size vegetable bundles can be enjoyed hot or cold.

1 tbsp. (15 ml) olive oil

1 onion, chopped

1 clove garlic, crushed

1 red or yellow pepper, seeded and diced

1 zucchini, diced

1½ cups (375 ml) chopped mushrooms

2 plum tomatoes, skinned, seeded, and chopped

1 tbsp. (15 ml) tomato paste

2 tbsp. (30 ml) chopped fresh basil

12 sheets (12 x 7 inches/13 x 18 cm) phyllo pastry dough, thawed if frozen

4 tbsp. (60 ml) butter, melted

1 Heat the oil in a saucepan, add the onion, garlic, pepper, zucchini, and mushrooms and cook gently for 10 minutes, stirring occasionally.

2 Remove from the heat, add the tomatoes, paste, and basil and stir to mix.

3 To make each bundle, cut each phyllo sheet in half crossways to make 2 squares (24 squares in total).

4 Lightly brush 2 phyllo squares with melted butter and place one on top of the other at diagonals. Spoon some filling into the center of the pastry dough.

5 Gather the dough up over the filling and tie loosely with string. Lightly brush with melted butter and place on a lightly greased baking sheet. Repeat with the remaining phyllo squares and filling to make a total of 12 bundles.

6 Bake the phyllo bundles in a preheated oven at 400°F (200°C) for 20–30 minutes, or until they are golden brown all over and nicely crisp.

7 Carefully remove and discard the string from each pastry bundle. Re-tie the parcels with fresh chives, if you like, for a decorative and edible effect.

❧

Variations

Top the vegetables with a little grated cheese before sealing the bundles.

Add some small cooked, shelled shrimp to the vegetables.

✿

Cook's Tips

To make a meal, serve with boiled new potatoes or mashed potatoes and broiled lean meat or chicken.

Instead of tying the tops of the dough bundles with string, gather the dough up over the filling and scrunch or fold to seal.

☆

Nutrition Notes

Vitamin C: ▲

✐

Useful Notes

: Yes : No

CAMPFIRE SAUSAGE KABOBS

PORTIONS: Makes 16 kebabs ❁ *PREPARATION TIME:* 20 minutes ❁ *COOKING TIME:* 15–20 minutes

Children love kabobs, and the combination of sausages, fruit, and vegetables make these particularly appealing. These are great to cook and serve at a family barbecue.

1 cup (250 ml) canned pineapple cubes in fruit juice

1 lb. (500 g) thin pork-and-herb link sausages

2 zucchini, each cut into 8 slices

1 red pepper, seeded and cut into 16 small squares

16 button mushrooms

1 tbsp. (15 ml) sunflower oil

2 tsp. (10 ml) whole-grain mustard

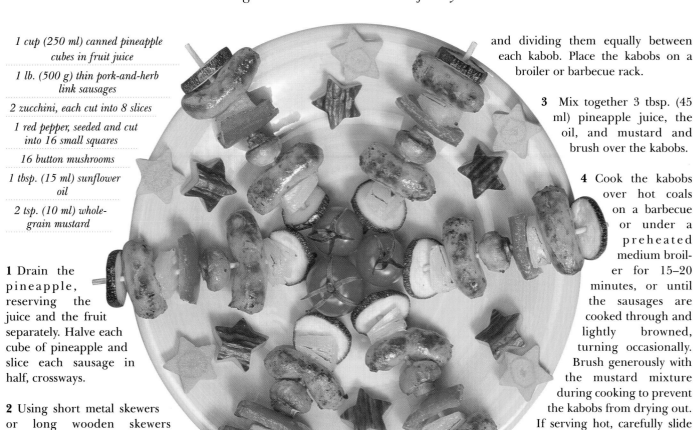

1 Drain the pineapple, reserving the juice and the fruit separately. Halve each cube of pineapple and slice each sausage in half, crossways.

2 Using short metal skewers or long wooden skewers snapped in half, thread the pineapple cubes, sausages, zucchini, pepper, and mushrooms onto the skewers, alternating the ingredients and dividing them equally between each kabob. Place the kabobs on a broiler or barbecue rack.

3 Mix together 3 tbsp. (45 ml) pineapple juice, the oil, and mustard and brush over the kabobs.

4 Cook the kabobs over hot coals on a barbecue or under a preheated medium broiler for 15–20 minutes, or until the sausages are cooked through and lightly browned, turning occasionally. Brush generously with the mustard mixture during cooking to prevent the kabobs from drying out. If serving hot, carefully slide the sausages, fruit, and vegetables onto plates before serving. The kabobs can also be served cold. Garnish with cherry tomatoes.

♥
Variations
Use other flavored thinly cut sausages, such as beef or spicy sausages, in place of the pork and herb sausages. Alternatively, use vegetarian sausages in place of the meat sausages.

Use low-fat sausages if you prefer for a healthier alternative.

❁
Cook's Tips
To make a meal, serve with fresh bread rolls and a rice or pasta salad.

Alternatively, serve the cooked kabob ingredients in finger rolls, hot-dog style.

For a vegetarian meal, use good-quality vegetarian sausages in place of the meat sausages.

★
Nutrition Notes
Vitamin C: ▲

✎
Useful Notes
❅: No   ❅: No

FROZEN RASPBERRY YOGURT

PORTIONS: Makes about 10 ✿ *PREPARATION TIME:* 15 minutes plus freezing time

A delicious, fruity, healthy alternative to ice cream, this homemade frozen yogurt is simple to make.

³/₄ lb. (350 g) raspberries

1¹/₄ cups (310 g) low-fat raspberry yogurt

1¹/₄ cups (310 g) whole-milk plain yogurt

¹/₄ cup (60 ml) sugar

1 Place the raspberries in a blender or food processor and blend until smooth. Press the fruit purée through a strainer, reserving the juice and pulp and discarding the seeds.

2 Return the raspberry juice and pulp to the rinsed-out food processor bowl. Add the raspberry yogurt, plain yogurt, and sugar and blend until well mixed.

3 Pour the mixture into a chilled, shallow, plastic container. Cover and freeze for 1¹/₂–2 hours, or until the mixture is mushy in consistency.

4 Turn into a chilled bowl and beat with a fork until smooth. Return to the container, cover, and freeze until firm.

Variations

Replace the raspberries with ³/₄ lb. (350 g) of one of the following: fresh blackberries, strawberries, mango, apricots, or peaches

Frozen raspberries work just as well in this recipe. Simply defrost and use as above.

✿

Cook's Tips

Use an ice-cream maker to make this yogurt ice. Follow individual manufacturer's directions.

Blend scoops of frozen yogurt with milk and extra fresh fruit for a refreshing thick milk shake.

5 Transfer to the refrigerator for 30 minutes before serving, to allow the frozen yogurt to soften a little. Serve in scoops in tall, decorative glasses. Serve with chopped fresh fruit and chocolate fingers for a special treat.

Serve this delicious frozen yogurt with extra fresh or canned fruit, such as melon or pineapple.

When you use sweeter fruit, such as strawberries or apricots for this frozen yogurt, reduce the amount of sugar added.

✩

Nutrition Notes

Calcium: ▲   *Vitamin C:* ▲

✐

Useful Notes

❄: *Yes*   ❄: *Yes*

MIXED BERRY MILK MOLDS

PORTIONS: Makes 6–8 small molds ✿ *PREPARATION TIME:* 10 minutes plus cooling and chilling time ✿ *COOKING TIME:* 5 minutes

These fruity milk molds will appeal to children of all ages, and are quick and easy to make.

1 standard box lemon-flavor gelatin

finely grated peel of 1 lemon

2 cups (500 ml) milk

¹/₂ lb. (250 g) fresh mixed berries, such as small strawberries, raspberries, and blackberries

1 Pour 1 cup (250 ml) hot water and 1 cup (250 ml) cold water into a bowl. Add the lemon-flavor gelatin to the water and stir to mix. Add the lemon peel and stir the gelatin mixture until the gelatin is thoroughly mixed with the water.

2 Gradually whisk in the milk, until the mixture is thoroughly blended.

3 Divide the fresh berries between individual dishes or molds or 1 large serving dish and pour the mixture over the fruit. Chill in the refrigerator until completely set.

4 If using molds, carefully unmold before serving, and serve the milk molds with lady fingers, if you like.

Variations

Omit the lemon peel and use different flavored gelatin, such as orange, strawberry, raspberry, or blackcurrant, in place of the lemon-flavor gelatin.

Use plain whole-milk yogurt in place of the milk.

✩

Nutrition Notes

Vitamin C: ▲▲

✐

Useful Notes

❄: *No*   ❄: *No*

CHOCOLATE-ORANGE ROULADE

PORTIONS: Makes 10 slices ✤ *PREPARATION TIME:* 20 minutes ✤ *COOKING TIME:* 10–15 minutes

A luxurious mixture of chocolate and orange, combined with a creamy yogurt filling, makes a dessert for any special occasion, but don't expect any leftovers!

3 eggs

½ cup (125 ml) sugar

⅔ cup (160 ml) all-purpose flour

1 tbsp. (15 ml) unsweetened cocoa powder

finely grated peel of 1 orange

2 tbsp. (30 ml) confectioners' sugar, sifted

⅔ cup (160 ml) crème fraîche (see page 73)

⅔ cup (160 ml) whole-milk plain yogurt

1 cup (250 ml) canned mandarin oranges in fruit juice, drained

1 Place the eggs and sugar in a large bowl and place the bowl over a pan of simmering water. Whisk, using an electric mixer, until the mixture is pale, creamy, and thick enough to leave a trail on the surface when the whisk is lifted.

2 Remove the bowl from the heat and whisk the egg mixture until very cool. Sift half the flour and cocoa powder over the mixture, then fold in gently using a metal spoon.

3 Sift over the remaining flour and cocoa powder and fold into the mixture with 1 tbsp. (15 ml) hot water.

4 Pour the mixture into a greased and lined 13 x 9 inch (33.5 x 22.5 cm) jelly roll pan, tilting the pan to level the surface.

5 Bake the roulade in a preheated oven at 400°F (200°C) for 10–15 minutes, or until the cake is well risen and firm to the touch.

6 Turn the cake out onto a sheet of nonstick baking paper, trim off the crusty edges, and quickly roll up the cake with the paper inside. Place seam-side down on a wire rack and allow to cool completely.

7 Once cooled, carefully unroll the cake. Mix together the orange peel and 1 tbsp. (15 ml) confectioners' sugar. Fold the crème fraîche, yogurt, and orange peel together and spread evenly over the cake. Scatter the mandarin oranges over the top of the cake.

8 Re-roll the cake, dust with the remaining sifted confectioners' sugar, and serve immediately in slices.

❧
Variations

For a plain roulade, replace the cocoa powder with all-purpose flour. Add the finely grated peel of 1 lemon or 1 orange to the plain mixture, if you like.

Spread the baked roulade with jam and thick cream for a special treat.

✎
Useful Notes

❀: Yes   ❀: Yes, but only the unfilled baked roulade

FRESH STRAWBERRY TARTLETTES

PORTIONS: Makes about 20 tartlettes ❂ *PREPARATION TIME:* 20 minutes plus 30 minutes chilling time ❂ *COOKING TIME:* 15–20 minutes

These fresh strawberry tartlettes look inviting and taste delicious!

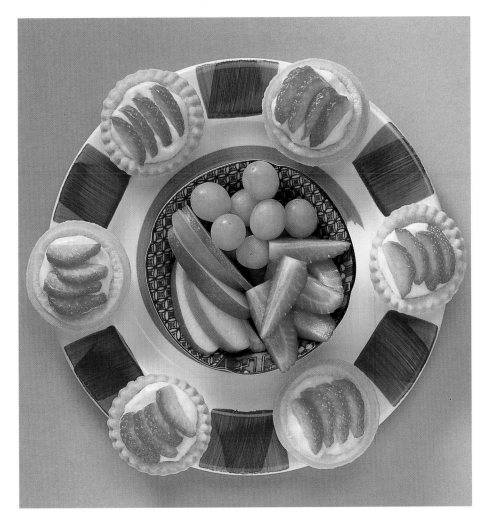

3 Roll out the dough on a lightly floured surface, cut into circles using a 3-inch (7.5-cm) plain cutter, and use to line about 20 small tartlette tins. Lightly prick the bases all over with a fork.

4 Bake in a preheated oven at 375°F (190°C) for 15–20 minutes, or until lightly browned. Allow the pastry shells to cool in the pans for 5 minutes, then carefully remove and place on a wire rack to cool completely.

5 Spoon the yogurt into the pastry shells. Top with strawberry halves or slices and serve immediately.

Variations

Use half white and half whole-wheat flours for the pastry dough.

Use small scoops of ice cream or frozen yogurt in place of the plain yogurt.

Serve with extra fresh strawberries or pieces or slices of other fresh fruits.

Cook's Tips

The fruit tartlettes can be glazed before serving, if you like. Simply heat a little strawberry or apricot jam until almost boiling, then carefully brush it evenly over the strawberries.

Serve with extra fresh fruit such as fresh fruit salad for a dessert.

Once made and cooled, store the pastry shells in an airtight container for several days. Fill and decorate just before serving.

Nutrition Notes

Vitamin C: ▲▲

Useful Notes

: *Yes*   ❂: *Yes, but only the unfilled cooked pastry cases*

---

1 cup (250 ml) plus 2 tbsp. (30 ml) all-purpose flour

pinch of salt

6 tbsp. (90 ml) butter or margarine

1¹/₃ cup (310 ml) whole-milk plain yogurt

¹/₂ lb. (250 g) strawberries, halved or sliced

1 To make the pastry dough, place the flour and salt in a bowl. Cut the butter or margarine lightly into the flour until the mixture resembles fine bread crumbs.

2 Mix in enough cold water to make a firm, smooth dough. Wrap in foil and chill in the refrigerator for 30 minutes.

MINI-CHOCOLATE CHIP MUFFINS

PORTIONS: Makes about 38 mini muffins ✪ *PREPARATION TIME:* 20 minutes ✪ *COOKING TIME:* 10–15 minutes

These mini muffins are the ideal little cakes for parties or picnics. Vary the flavor by replacing the chocolate chips with chopped dried or fresh fruit. They can be served warm or cold.

1¹/₃ cups (310 ml) all-purpose flour

1 tbsp. (15 ml) baking powder

pinch of salt

4 tbsp. (60 ml) butter or margarine, melted

¹/₄ cup (60 ml) sugar

1 egg

³/₄ cup (180 ml) plus 2 tbsp. (30 ml) milk

³/₄ cup (187 ml) semisweet chocolate chips

1 Sift the flour, baking powder, and salt into a bowl. Mix together the melted butter or margarine, sugar, egg, and milk and pour over the dry ingredients.

2 Gently fold the ingredients together, only enough to combine the mixture.

The mixture will look quite lumpy—over-mixing will result in heavy muffins.

3 Gently fold in the chocolate chips, then spoon the mixture into paper mini muffin cases laid out on 2 baking sheets, filling each case two-thirds full.

4 Bake in a preheated oven at 400°F (200°C) for 10–15 minutes or until well risen and golden brown.

5 Transfer to a wire rack to cool.

Variations

Replace the chocolate chips with ³/₄ cup (187 ml) of one of the following: milk or white chocolate chips; raisins or golden raisins; finely chopped ready-to-eat dried apricots, peaches, pears, pineapple, or dates; frozen raspberries or blackberries; small fresh blueberries; fresh chopped strawberries, apples, or pears.

✿
Cook's Tips

Muffins are best eaten fresh on the day they are made.

Once cool, store in an airtight container for up to 2 days. Warm in a low oven before serving, if you like.

✎
Useful Notes

❀: Yes   ❄: Yes

APPLE AND SPICE BARS

PORTIONS: Makes 16 bars ❀ PREPARATION TIME: 20 minutes ❀ COOKING TIME: 35–40 minutes

These fruity bars make a favorite and easily portable finger food for a picnic or outdoor party.

¹/₂ cup (125 ml) butter or margarine, softened

¹/₂ cup (125 ml) light soft brown sugar

2 eggs, beaten

³/₄ cup (180 ml) self-rising white flour

³/₄ cup (180 ml) wholemeal flour

1¹/₂ tsp (7.5 ml) apple pie spice

1 medium cooking apple, peeled, cored, and chopped

³/₄ cup (187 ml) golden raisins

a little milk, to mix

1 Cream the butter or margarine and sugar together until pale and fluffy. Gradually add the beaten eggs, beating well after each addition.

2 Fold in the flours and spice and mix thoroughly. Fold in the apples, golden raisins, and enough milk to make the mixture a soft, dropping consistency.

3 Turn into a lightly greased 7 x 11 inch (17.5 x 27.5 cm) baking pan and level.

4 Bake in a preheated oven at 350°F (180°C) for 35–40 minutes, or until risen, golden brown, and firm to the touch.

5 Cool in the pan for a few minutes, then mark into bars and turn out onto a wire rack to cool completely.

Variation

Use 1 large pear in place of the apple.

✿
Cook's Tips

Serve these fruity bars warm or cold with ice cream for a dessert.

Once cool, store in an airtight container.

✎
Useful Notes

❀: Yes   ❄: Yes

FRUITY OATMEAL SQUARES

PORTIONS: Makes 24–36 oatmeal squares ✿ *PREPARATION TIME:* 15 minutes ✿ *COOKING TIME:* 25–30 minutes

Easy to make, these satisfying squares will be enjoyed by toddlers and adults alike.

½ cup (125 ml) butter or margarine

¼ cup (60 ml) light soft brown sugar

4 tbsp. (60 ml) clear honey

1½ cups (375 ml) quick-cooking oatmeal

⅓ cup (80 ml) porridge oats

1 tsp. (5 ml) ground cinnamon or apple pie spice

½ cup (125 ml) chopped ready-to-eat dried pears

½ cup (125 ml) finely chopped ready-to-eat dried pineapple

1 Place the butter or margarine, sugar, and honey in a saucepan and heat gently until melted, stirring continuously. Pour onto the oatmeal and oats and stir to mix. Add the cinnamon or apple pie spice and dried fruit and mix well.

2 Turn the mixture into a lightly greased, shallow 6-inch (15-cm) square cake pan and level the surface with a metal spatula.

3 Bake in a preheated oven at 350°F (180°C) for 25–30 minutes, or until golden brown.

4 Cool slightly in the pan, then mark into small squares using a sharp knife. Loosen the squares around the edges of the pan.

5 When firm, cut into squares, and remove from the pan. Transfer to a wire rack to cool completely.

Useful Notes
❄: Yes ✿: Yes

MINI-APRICOT BISCUITS

PORTIONS: Makes about 32 mini-biscuits ✿ *PREPARATION TIME:* 20 minutes ✿ *COOKING TIME:* 8–10 minutes

These delicious mini biscuits are an ideal toddler size! Serve warm or cold.

1½ cups (375 ml) self-rising flour

1 tsp. (5 ml) baking powder

pinch of salt

4 tbsp. (60 ml) butter or margarine

¾ cup (180 ml) finely chopped ready-to-eat dried apricots

about ⅔ cup (160 ml) milk

1 Sift the flour, baking powder, and salt into a bowl. Lightly cut in the butter or margarine until the mixture resembles fine bread crumbs. Stir in the apricots.

2 Make a well in the center and stir in enough milk to make a soft dough.

3 Turn the dough onto a lightly floured surface, knead gently, and roll or pat out lightly until about ½ inch (2.5 cm) thick. Cut into circles or squares using a 1-inch (2.5-cm) cutter or sharp knife and place on a lightly floured baking sheet.

4 Bake in a preheated oven at 425°F (220°C) for 8–10 minutes, or until well risen and golden brown.

5 Transfer to a wire rack to cool. Serve on their own or split and spread with butter or margarine, jam, or honey.

✿
Cook's Tips

When making biscuits and mixing the ingredients together, never overmix or knead the mixture too heavily because this can result in heavy, uneven biscuits.

Do not roll the dough out too thinly because this can also result in heavy, uneven biscuits.

Useful Notes
❄: Yes ✿: Yes

QUICK-AND-DELICIOUS MILK SHAKE

PORTIONS: Makes about 2 cups (500 ml)   *PREPARATION TIME:* 5 minutes

Children will often take milk as a drink when combined with other foods, particularly fruit.
Try some of these ideas to tempt toddlers to a nutritious drink at partytime.

¹/₄ cups (310 ml) milk

1 medium banana, peeled and sliced

2 scoops soft scoop vanilla ice cream
or frozen yogurt

1 Place the milk, banana, and ice cream or frozen yogurt in a blender or food processor. Blend for 10–20 seconds or until smooth, well mixed, and frothy.

2 Pour the milk shake into decorative glasses and serve immediately.

Variations

Use ¹/₂ cup (125 ml) other fresh or canned fruit, such as strawberries, apricots, peaches, pineapple, or mixed fruit salad, in place of the banana.

Use ²/₃ cup (60 ml) fruit yogurt in place of the ice cream or frozen yogurt.

For a fizzy shake, use lemonade or soda water in place of the milk. Simply blend the milk with the fruit and ice cream as above, pour into a glass, and top up with lemonade or soda water.

For a yogurt shake, use whole-milk plain or flavored yogurt in place of the milk.

Cook's Tips

If you don't have a blender or food processor, simply mash the banana with a fork and then, using an electric mixer or hand whisk, beat the mashed fruit, milk, and ice cream together until the mixture is smooth and thoroughly mixed.

Nutrition Notes

Calcium: ▲

Useful Notes

❀: Yes ✿: No

121

NUTRITIONAL BREAKDOWN OF RECIPES

Full nutritional information has not been included for the recipes in Chapter 1, because this first stage of weaning is more concerned with developing tastes and textures than about providing extra nutrients. However, we have highlighted those recipes in the chapter that contain useful or rich sources of some essential vitamins and minerals.

The nutritional information has been compiled per 100g of the recipe, with a few exceptions, because individual portion sizes will vary considerably, depending on a variety of factors. The values given are approximate.

	Energy kcal	Protein	Carbohydrate	Fat	of which saturates	Fiber	Sodium	Iron	Vitamin C	Calcium
Beef and Vegetable Casserole *page 42*	101	8.1g	2.5g	6.6g	2.7g	0.8g	0.06g	1.4mg	6.4mg	
Cheesy Cod and Zucchini Supper *page 42*	88	6.6g	4.7g	5.0g	2.1g	0.3g	0.07g			63mg
Summer Vegetable Medley *page 44*	54	1.3g	5.8g	3.1g	0.7g	0.5g	0.1g		13mg	
Pasta with Tuna, Spinach, and Cream Cheese *page 45*	128	9.9g	7.4g	6.7g	3.0g	0.9g	0.2g			
Creamy Lentil Hotpot *page 46*	43	2.9g	7.0g	0.6g	0.3g	1.5g	0.03g		7.2mg	
Stir-Fried Chicken with Avocado and Rice *page 46*	88	5.2g	8.8g	3.8g	0.7g	0.7g	0.2g			
Ham and Pepper Scramble *page 48*	146	10.0g	1.5g	11.2g	3.7g	0.7g	0.3g	1.3mg	17.8mg	
Bean and Vegetable Bake *page 49*	115	5.6g	12.7g	4.9g	2.5g	2.7g	0.2g			101mg
Potato, Leek, and Cheese Pie *page 50*	145	7.4g	10.5g	8.4g	5.1g	1.5g	0.2g		10mg	172mg
Macaroni and Cheese with Broccoli *page 50*	126	5.4g	11.1g	7.0g	3.6g	0.7g	0.1g		10.3mg	116mg
Plum and Lemon Rice Dessert *page 52*	63	2.1g	8.2g	2.7g	1.5g	0.2g	0.03g			
Poached Plum and Pear Compote *page 53*	35	0.3g	8.8g	0.1g	0.0g	1.0g	0.02g			
Stewed Apple with Cinnamon *page 53*	62	0.5g	15.7g	0.1g	0.0g	1.6g	3.1g			
Raspberry Delight *page 54*	81	1.6g	18.6g	0.4g	0.3g	0.0g	12.5mg	0.3mg	7.8mg	
Mango with Yogurt *page 54*	72	1.9g	13.9g	1.2g	0.6g	0.6g	29.4mg		11.4mg	52.8mg
Peach and Raspberry Fool *page 56*	49	1.5g	9.3g	1.1g	0.5g	1.0g	14mg	0.3mg	9.3mg	41.8mg
Apricot Yogurt Fool *page 57*	52	1.4g	8.4g	9.0g	0.5g	1.1g	13.9mg	5.8mg	6.9mg	39.2mg
Spring Vegetable Omelet *page 62*	118	7.4g	3.4g	8.4g	3.5g	1.3g	0.1g		21mg	104mg
Turkey Stir-Fry *page 63*	82	8.0g	5.5g	3.2g	0.5g	1.0g	0.06g		30mg	

	Energy kcal	Protein	Carbohydrate	Fat	of which saturates	Fiber	Sodium	Iron	Vitamin C	Calcium
Mini Meatballs in Herby Tomato Sauce *page 64*	109	11.8g	4.9g	4.8g	1.1g	0.6g	0.1g			
Spaghetti and Sauce *page 65*	112	8.6g	4.9g	6.6g	2.8g	1.0g	0.09g	1.5mg	9.1mg	
Salmon and Herb Fish Cakes with Tomato Salsa *page 66*	95	6.2g	8.0g	4.5g	1.2g	0.8g	0.2g		6.6mg	
Baked Cod with Cheese and Corn Sauce *page 67*	91	9.8g	3.1g	4.5g	2.2g	0.3g	0.2g			78mg
Sweet Potato and Chick-Pea Bake *page 68*	126	3.9g	13.1g	6.8g	2.4g	1.9g	0.1g		11mg	74mg
Pasta Twists with Zucchini and Peppers *page 69*	95	3.8g	15.6	2.3g	0.3g	2.4g	0.07g		14.8mg	
Mixed Bean and Vegetable Risotto *page 70*	113	4.3g	23.1g	1.0g	0.2g	2.4g	0.07g	1.2mg	16mg	
Fresh Mushroom Soup *page 71*	105	3.6g	7.9g	6.7g	2.9g	1.1g	83mg		14mg	96mg
Strawberry-Yogurt Gelatin *page 72*	85	2.6g	14.7g	1.4g	0.8g	0.4g	38mg	2.7mg	10.6mg	52mg
Chocolate-Banana Whip *page 73*	167	2.9g	20.1g	8.8g	5.3g	0.5g	38mg			
Cherry Batter Dessert *page 74*	128	2.5g	22.3g	3.9g	0.6g	0.8g	19.4mg	2.6mg		
Mixed Fruit Compote *page 75*	36	0.7g	8.5g	0.2g	0.0g	1.5g	0.00g		30mg	
Pear and Apricot Pudding *page 76*	187	4.1g	40.1g	1.9g	0.5g	1.9g	0.1g			
Strawberry Rice Pudding *page 77*	77	2.6g	7.4g	3.8g	2.3g	0.6g	31.9mg		6mg	80mg
Chicken Fingers with Barbecue Sauce *page 84*	94	9.5g	9.3g	2.3g	0.6g	0.1g	0.09g			
Chicken, Leek, and Potato Hash *page 85*	138	9.6g	7.8g	7.9g	1.3g	1.3g	0.03g		19.7mg	
Wild West Vegetable Chili Tacos *page 86*	93	4.2g	10.7g	4.0g	1.7g	2.4g	0.2g	0.9mg	25mg	88mg
Tuna Lasgne *page 87*	151	9.9g	13.4g	6.8g	3.5g	0.7g	0.2g		8.4mg	117mg
Spinach and Hamburgers *page 88*	151	12.1g	3.8g	9.8g	4.0g	0.8g	0.2g	2.0mg		
Stuffed Zucchini *page 89*	185	8.5g	2.7g	15.7g	6.2g	0.8g	0.3g		24mg	173mg
Sweet-and-Sour Rice Salad *page 90*	70	1.8g	15.4g	0.6g	0.1g	0.9g	0.2g		18mg	
Mild Vegetable Curry with Couscous *page 90*	78	3.3g	15.5g	0.7g	0.1g	2.3g	0.02g	1.7g	20mg	
Pepper, Leek, and Potato Frittata *page 92*	134	6.9g	6.3g	9.1g	3.4g	0.9g	0.1g	0.9mg	15mg	95mg
Herby Shrimp and Mushroom Pilaf *page 92*	120	8.1g	20.1g	1.3g	0.3g	2.0g	0.3g			
Chunky Vegetable Soup *page 93*	73	2.2g	8.6g	3.6g	0.5g	2.7g	0.02g	1.0mg	14mg	
Egg and Tomato Topper *page 94*	124	7.2g	2.4g	9.6g	2.3g	0.5g	0.1g	1.2mg	8.6mg	
Cheese and Carrot Topper *page 94*	268	13.3g	15.5g	17.4g	10.9g	1.1g	0.3g			376mg
Tuna and Corn Topper *page 94*	171	13.7g	12.4g	7.8g	1.3g	0.6g	0.3g	1.0mg		

	Energy kcal	Protein	Carbohydrate	Fat	of which saturates	Fiber	Sodium	Iron	Vitamin C	Calcium
Smoked Ham and Tomato Topper *page 94*	61	5.2g	7.1g	1.5g	0.5g	0.8g	0.3g		11mg	
Apricot Coleslaw Topper *page 94*	89	2.1g	12.3g	3.8g	0.7g	2.9g	0.04g	1.1mg	19mg	
Pear-Chocolate Upside-Down Pudding *page 96*	212	3.8g	28.9g	9.8g	3.8g	1.3g	0.2mg			88mg
Banana Cheesecake *page 97*	271	6.0g	16.0g	2.3g	7.6g	0.2g	1.7mg		5.6mg	28mg
Baked Fruit Bonanza *page 98*	54	0.8g	13.1g	0.2g	0.0g	1.4g	2.4g		16mg	
Hot Lemon Soufflé *page 98*	186	6.1g	20.3g	9.5g	3.5g	0.2g	0.1g			
Summer Fruit Salad *page 99*	43	0.7g	10.4g	0.1g	0.0g	1.1g	0.06g		25.8mg	
Banana Tea Loaf *page 100*	239	4.0g	37.8g	9.0g	2.9g	2.3g	0.1g			
Carrot and Golden Raisin Fingers *page 101*	334	3.6g	44.7g	16.9g	5.5g	1.4g	0.2g			
Apple and Apricot Crumble *page 101*	129	1.5g	21.2g	4.8g	1.5g	1.6g	0.05g		8mg	
Fun Pizza Faces *page 106*	241	7.9g	24.2g	3.2g	5.6g	2.3g	0.3g		13.7g	185mg
Chicken and Sesame Nuggets *page 107*	228	24.8g	11.9g	9.3g	2.0g	2.2g	0.2mg	2.7mg	14.8mg	
Tuna and Avocado Pasta Salad *page 108*	151	8.1g	16.5g	6.3g	1.2g	2.3g	0.1g	1.4mg	13.6mg	
Cheese Twists *page 109*	384	12.6	28.8g	25.1g	10.1g	1.1g	0.3g			257mg
Cheese and Ham Whirls *page 110*	267	10.0g	27.7g	13.7g	6.0g	1.4g	0.5g			260mg
Pinwheel Sandwiches *page 110 (figures per sandwich)*	19	0.96g	2.0g	0.7g	0.3g	0.3g	59.6mg	0.16mg	0.66mg	5mg
Zebra Sandwiches *page 110*	196	3.8g	34.0g	6.0g	1.9g	1.9g	0.3g			
Mediterranean Vegetable Bundles *page 112*	316	2.8g	15.4g	27.5g	12.5g	1.3g	0.3g		15.6mg	
Campfire Sausage Kabobs *page 113*	233	6.1g	9.0g	19.4g	6.8g	0.7g	0.4g		11mg	
Frozen Raspberry Yogurt *page 114*	83	2.3	16.0g	1.3g	0.8g	0.8g	28.5mg		6.3mg	79mg
Mixed Berry Milk Molds *page 114*	89	3.0g	15.2g	2.2g	1.4g	0.3g	0.04g		22mg	73mg
Chocolate-Orange Roulade *page 116 (figures per slice)*	148	4.7g	22.0g	4.7g	2.5g	0.3g	36.3mg	0.7mg	9mg	29.4mg
Fresh Strawberry Tartlettes *page 117 (figures per tartlette)*	76	1.5g	6.5g	5.0g	3.0g	0.05g	41.3mg	0.38mg	4.3mg	6mg
Mini-Chocolate Chip Muffins *page 118*	349	6.3g	50.6g	14.9g	6.4g	1.0g	0.4g			
Apple and Spice Bars *page 119*	310	5.0g	45.5g	13.2g	4.2g	2.3g	0.2g			
Fruity Oatmeal Squares *page 120*	408	3.5g	47.2g	24.1g	7.6g	3.1g	0.4g			
Mini-Apricot Biscuits *page 120*	313	6.4g	47.2g	12.2g	4.3g	2.8g	0.3g			
Quick-and-Delicious Milk Shake *page 121*	85	2.6g	12.0g	3.3g	2.1g	0.3g	0.03g			83mg

apples
  and apricot crumble 101
  and spice bars 119
  stewed with cinnamon 53
  stewed with pears 33
  and strawberry purée 35
apricots
  and apple crumble 101
  and banana purée 32
  and mango purée 36
  mini-biscuits 120
  and pear purée 33
  and pear pudding 76-7
  yogurt fool 57
avocado
  with chick-peas 31
  and melon purée 37
  stir-fried chicken with rice 46-7
  and tuna pasta salad 108

baby rice 18
  and butter beans 28
  and mashed banana 35
  mashed carrots and peas 29
  with mashed cauliflower 23
  and nectarine purée 34
  and zucchini 23
bananas
  and apricot purée 32
  cheesecake 97
  chocolate whip 73
  mashed with baby rice 35
  with plums 37
  tea loaf 100
beans
  and vegetable bake 49
  and vegetable risotto 70
  zucchini and cheese purée 29
beef
  ground with carrot and potato 30
  stock 14
  and vegetable casserole 42
berry milk molds 114
broccoli
  with macaroni and cheese 50-1
  and potato purée 25
butter beans and baby rice 28

carrots
  and cauliflower purée 26
  mashed with peas and baby rice 29
  with mashed potatoes 22
  and golden raisin fingers 101
  ground beef and potato 30
  and turnip purée 24
cauliflower
  and carrots purée 26
  mashed with baby rice 23
cheese 50-1, 67
  green bean and zucchini purée 29
  and ham whirls 110
  with mixed vegetables 31
  potato and leek pie 50
  twists 109
cherry batter dessert 74-5
chicken
  fingers with barbecue sauce 84-5
  leek and potato hash 85
  and sesame nuggets 107
  stir-fried with avocado 46-7
  stock 14
chick-peas
  with avocado 31
  and sweet potato bake 68
chocolate
  banana-whip 73
  mini-muffins 118-9
  orange roulade 116
  pear upside-down pudding 96-7
cod
  with cheese and corn 67
  and zucchini supper 42-3

fruit 34, 75, 98, 99
fruity oatmeal squares 120

ham 48, 110
hamburgers, spinach and 88

leeks
  chicken and potato hash 85
  peppers and potato frittata 92
  potato and cheese pie 50
lemon soufflé 98
lentils 30, 46

mangoes
  and apricot purée 36
  with yogurt 54-5
meatballs in herby tomato sauce 64
melons
  and avocado purée 37
  with peaches 36
  milkshake 121
mushrooms
  and shrimp pilaf 92
  soup 71
  and sweet potato purée 24

parties 102-21
pasta
  macaroni and cheese with broccoli 50-1
  spaghetti and sauce 65
  tuna and avocado salad 108
  tuna lasagne 87
  with tuna, spinach, and cream cheese 45
  with zucchini and peppers 69
peaches
  with mashed pears 32
  with melons 36
  and raspberry fool 56
pears
  and apricot purée 33
  and apricot pudding 76-7
  chocolate upside-down pudding 96-7
  mashed with peaches 32
  and poached plum compote 53
  and stewed apples 33
peas
  mashed carrots and baby rice 29
  and potato purée 27
peppers
  and ham scramble 48
  leek and potato frittata 92
  pasta twists with zucchini 69
picnics 102-21
pizza faces 106-7
plums
  with banana 37
  and lemon rice dessert 52
  and pear compote 53
potatoes
  baked 94
  and broccoli purée 25

ground beef with carrot 30
chicken and leek hash 85
leek and cheese pie 50
mashed with carrots 22
mashed with greens 26
and pea purée 27
pepper and leek frittata 92

raspberries
  delight 54
  frozen yogurt 114
  and peach fool 56
rice 46-7, 52, 77, 90

salmon and herb fish cakes 66-7
sandwiches 110-1
sausages, campfire kabobs 113
shrimp and mushroom pilaf 92
spaghetti and sauce 65
spinach
  and hamburgers 88
  pasta with tuna and cream cheese 45
stocks 14
strawberries
  and apple purée 35
  rice pudding 77
  tartlettes 117
  yogurt gelatin 72
sweet potato
  and chick-pea bake 68
  and mushroom purée 24

toast toppers 94
tuna
  and avocado pasta salad 108
  lasagne 87
  pasta with spinach and cream cheese 45
turkey stir-fry 63
turnip and carrot purée 24

vegetables 22, 25, 27, 31, 42, 44, 86, 90, 93, 112

zucchini
  and baby rice 23
  and cheesy cod supper 42-3
  green bean and cheese purée 29
  pasta twists with peppers 69
  stuffed 89